Cont

General themes

Christian calendar events

10-minute assemblies for 4-11s

50 ready-to-use assemblies exploring values from a Christian perspective

Rebecca Parkinson

For all the staff and children who have made my time as a teacher such a wonderful experience. With particular thanks to Janice Porter for all her encouragement.

Acknowledgements

It is a great privilege to have the opportunity to visit so many schools and to see the great work carried out by the staff and children. I would particularly like to thank all the children who have taken part in my assemblies, informing me of the things that worked well and those that needed to be changed. Thank you for your honesty!

Thanks as always to Ted, Anna and Lydia, for always being there for me.

Special thanks to my mum and dad for their constant help and encouragement.

National days

Other annual or special events

Introduction

If you have ever been asked to lead a whole school or class assembly or prepare a children's talk for a church service, or if you are looking for fresh ideas for lessons, this is the book for you! *10-Minute Assemblies for 4–11s* provides 50 ready-to-use, thought-provoking assemblies that will immediately grab the children's attention. The ideas are quick and easy to use and cover many general themes alongside Christian calendar events, national days and other annual or special events. (The general themes and special events are presented in alphabetical order, not in the order that you would necessarily use them through the year.)

All the assemblies have been tried and tested with children and the inclusion of an optional Bible section makes them suitable for use in any school. The assemblies are designed to be flexible and easy to use for teachers with little or no Christian background knowledge. All you will need is a Bible or a printout of the relevant verses from www.biblegateway.com in a modern translation such as the New International Version, the Good News Bible or the Contemporary English Version.

Age ranges

The assemblies are written to be used in Key Stages 1 and 2 but could easily be adapted to suit slightly younger or older ages.

Group sizes

All the assemblies are suitable for whole school usage but, with minimum effort, could be adapted for use as classroom assemblies or in any lessons or talks involving children. For larger groups, there may be occasions when it is necessary to duplicate some of the suggested pieces of equipment so that more children can be actively involved.

Organisation

A number of the assemblies require the involvement of two or more people. On these occasions, pre-planning is particularly important so that each person is sure of the role they are playing.

General themes

1

All in this together

Aim: To consider that each of us is vitally important in keeping the peace and promoting team spirit within school.

You will need: A long paper chain with links of different sizes, colours, widths and lengths; a bag or box; a paper chain with each link identical (optional).

To make the chain, cut lots of strips of paper of different shapes, colours and sizes. Bend one strip into a circle and stick or staple the ends together. Pass another strip through the loop and stick the ends of the second strip together. Continue passing strips through the loops until a long chain is formed. The longer you can make your chain, the better. The chain should be placed in the bag or box so that it remains unseen until needed.

The chain with identical links could be used for comparison with the main chain, emphasising that our differences make us far more interesting and special.

Assembly outline

Explain to the children that you have made something special for today's assembly. Point out that it took you a long time to make and that it needs handling with care. Ask for a volunteer to help you, and invite that child to stand near the box containing the chain. Lift the lid of the box slowly, trying to build up the tension among the children. Ask the volunteer to pull the end of the chain slowly. As it unravels, look excited and surprised that the chain is so long. Once the whole chain has been unravelled, ask for a number of volunteers to hold it so that everyone can see.

Ask the children to look carefully at the chain and say what they notice about it. Children will comment that all the links are different. Ask for a number of volunteers to come forward and each describe two or three of the links in the chain. Their descriptions might be that one link is gold in colour, very long, thin and shiny, while another is pink, short, wide and dull, and so on. You may want to ask the children to choose their favourites.

Explain that, as you made the chain, you were thinking about all the children in school. Just as every link in the chain is different, so each child in the school is different. It is our differences that make us so special and interesting. (If the optional paper chain with identical links has been made, show this chain and ask the children which they like more. You hope they will say the first chain!)

Ask the children at the two ends of the chain to keep hold of it while the others carefully let go. Ask the two children at the ends to hold the chain as high as they can. Explain that you are going to do something that will spoil the chain. As you speak, break one of the links so that the broken ends fall to the floor. Explain that it only took a small action to ruin the chain. It was only one link that was damaged, but it affected the whole chain. Every link, whether big or small, is important.

Explain that, in the same way, it only takes one person in school to do something that 'breaks' the care/peace/harmony of the school. The actions of just one person can make things fall apart.

Remind the children that in school we are like a team. We are all there to look after each other, care for each other and support each other. If one of us decides not to do this, all of us are affected in some way. Each of us has a part to play in keeping the peace and promoting team spirit within school.

Challenge the children to think of themselves as an important link in the school.

This assembly works well if the children are allowed to write their names on the chain during the course of the day and the chain is then placed at the front of the hall or classroom as a reminder that we all matter.

What the Bible says

When Jesus was on earth, he knew how important it was to be part of a team. As soon as he began to move across the country, carrying out miracles and teaching people about God, he gathered a team of people around himself. These special friends were known as his disciples. The disciples went with him wherever he went, helping him and caring for him.

To most people, Jesus would have appeared to be more important than his disciples. However, on one special occasion Jesus showed how important he thought the disciples were. In **John 13:1–17** we read a beautiful story about Jesus kneeling down and washing the disciples' dirty feet. If we are going to work as a team in school, we need to realise that everybody is as important as everybody else, and we need to treat others with respect and love.

Pause for thought

Think for a moment about the way in which you treat other people. Do you treat them in a respectful, kind, thoughtful way? Is there anything you could do to help everyone in school stay together as a team? Do you need to make friends with anyone? Do you need to say sorry to anyone? Remember, it is all the little links in a chain that hold it together.

PRAYER
Dear God, please help us to realise that we all have an important role to play in making our school a safe, caring and happy place to be. Please help us to think about other people as we learn to live together in the world. Amen

2

Beauty on the inside

Aim: To consider that beauty on the inside is more important than the way we appear on the outside.

If possible, ask a member of staff if they would be willing to have a 'makeover' during the assembly. If you know a beautician, you could invite them in to help carry out the makeover. You may want to ask the staff member to bring in some 'posh' clothes to demonstrate what they might wear if they were going out somewhere—the more glamorous, the better.

You will need: Face wipes to enable the staff member to remove the make-up; or (if a staff member is unavailable) a selection of materials designed to improve our looks, such as shower gel, lipstick, mascara, false nails, hair gel, 'going out' clothes and jewellery.

Assembly outline

Invite the prearranged staff member to come forward. Point out that, as this person comes into work each day, everyone is used to their appearance; everyone recognises who they are because their appearance stays largely the same. Say that this is true for all the other members of staff and the pupils at the school: they all have a similar appearance day after day.

Ask the children what they think the staff member would do differently if they were going out to a wedding. Allow them time to answer. They will probably suggest make-up, new clothes and other similar things.

Explain that you (or your visiting beautician) are going to carry out a 'makeover' on the staff member.

Or:

Explain to the children that you want them to imagine that all the teachers in school are going out for a meal this evening to celebrate something good that has happened. They are going to visit an expensive restaurant. Ask the children to imagine what the teachers will do when they get home from school tonight. As they make suggestions, such as 'have a shower' or 'put on make-up', invite them forward to hold up the appropriate items—hair gel, shower gel, lipstick and so on.

Having carried out one of the activities above, ask the children if the person who has had the makeover looks any different, *or* ask if the staff members who dress up for tonight's meal will look different from how they look at the present time. After some discussion, ask the children if the teachers will actually be any different on the inside.

Explain that we can all make ourselves look different on the outside but that doesn't change the person we really are deep down. Point out that often we are very quick to judge people by what we see on the outside. We look at their clothes, toys, hairstyle or similar things, and use these things to decide if we want to be friends with that person or even if that person is worth speaking to. By doing this, though, we can easily miss out on getting to know some amazing people.

What the Bible says

In **1 Samuel 16:1–12**, the prophet Samuel is choosing the person who will become the future king of Israel. He visits the home of a father called Jesse, who parades each of his sons before Samuel. Although they are described as handsome, strong and good fighters, God tells Samuel that these men are not his choice for the king.

Eventually Jesse asks his youngest son, David, to appear before Samuel. David is only a young boy but God speaks to Samuel and says that David will one day be the king of Israel. The key verse in the passage is verse 7, which says, 'People look at the outward appearance, but the Lord looks at the heart.'

Pause for thought

How important do you think it is to look good on the outside? Are you more likely to want to make friends with someone who wears expensive clothes, lives in a big house and has lots of money than with someone who does not?

Let's remember that the way people look on the outside does not tell us what they are really like inside. Let's take the time to get to know other people, no matter what their outward appearance is like.

PRAYER

Dear God, thank you for everything that we have. Thank you for our clothes and our homes. We ask you to help those who have much less than we do. Please help us to remember that it is far more important to be good people on the inside than to look good on the outside. Help us always to take the time to get to know people, rather than judging them by what we see. Amen

3

Being lights

Aim: To consider that we can all be lights that make a difference in the world.

You will need: A 'feely bag' with a variety of objects in it; a number of objects that give out light.

Your feely bag could contain, for example, a chocolate biscuit, a piece of uncooked pasta, a pen lid and a memory stick—some items that will be easy to guess and others that will be harder. Objects that give out light could include a torch, a mobile phone, glow sticks and a lamp.

Assembly outline

Ask the children to shut their eyes and remain quiet for 20 seconds. While their eyes are shut, carry out a number of actions. (Remember that some of the children will be peeping, so turn away while you do it.) Examples could be to pull a funny face, do an impression of an animal, eat something or make a clapping action without sound.

Once the children have opened their eyes, ask if they can tell you what actions you made while their eyes were closed. Explain that sometimes our eyes are closed, so we can't see what is going on around us, but sometimes we can't see something even when our eyes are open.

Show the children the feely bag and ask for a volunteer to guess one of the objects inside it. Ask the child to place their hand inside the bag, choose an object, describe to the other children how it feels, and then guess what it is. If they guess correctly, they should remove the object. Repeat with different volunteers until all the objects have been guessed. Alternatively, you could ask a child to feel an object and then describe it so that the other children can guess what it is.

Ask for a number of volunteers, equivalent to the number of light-giving objects you have available. Give each child an object and ask the others to say what all the objects have in common. Ask them if they can think of anything else that gives out light: examples might be fire, street lights and so on.

Remind the children that sometimes we can't see because our eyes are closed, and sometimes we can't see because something forms a barrier between us and the object, such as a feely bag or a wall. Sometimes, however, we can't see because it is dark.

Ask the children if they have ever been in a place where there was absolutely no light. Invite them to describe what it was like and how they felt. Ask them if they have ever been outside at night in an area where there are no street lights. Invite them to describe the night sky and how many stars can be seen in it. If the children have no experience of either of these situations, describe your own experiences.

Ask the children if they have ever felt sad or lonely. Explain that everyone, at some time in their lives, feels like this. It may be that someone close to them has died, they have fallen out with a friend, they are ill, they have to do things that they don't want to do, or they feel that they are being bullied. Ask the children what made them feel better when they felt like this. It may be that someone has made them laugh, given them a hug or simply looked after them.

Explain that when we are sad and down in the dumps, it can feel as if we are in the dark on the inside. However, when people have cheered us up, it can feel as if a light has shone into our lives. It is a bit like being in the dark, feeling worried or afraid, when suddenly a light is switched on, and immediately everything feels better.

Explain that many people in the world feel sad and alone, as if their world is dark. The wonderful thing is that all of us can be 'lights' in other people's lives. Sometimes even something as simple as a smile or a kind word can cheer someone up and make them feel much better.

What the Bible says

In **Matthew 5—7** we read the famous collection of Jesus' teachings called the Sermon on the Mount. In **Matthew 5:14–16**, Jesus describes his followers as the 'light of the world' and goes on to say that our lights should shine out to other people. You may like to ask a child to read this passage from the Bible:

You are the light of the world. A town built on a hill cannot be hidden. Neither do people light a lamp and put it under a bowl. Instead they put it on its stand, and it gives light to everyone in the house. In the same way, let your light shine before others, that they may see your good deeds and glorify your Father in heaven.

Jesus also describes himself as 'the light of the world', in **John 8:12**.

Pause for thought

Can you think of a time when you felt sad and someone cheered you up? At that moment someone brought light back into your life. Do you know someone who is sad today? What could you do to bring light into their situation? Why not look out today for people whom you could cheer up? Remember that even a smile is a very powerful light.

PRAYER

Dear God, thank you for all the people who make us happy. Thank you for people who care for us when we are sad and feeling down in the dumps. Please help us to be lights in the lives of others. Help us to take the time to notice when others are sad and to be sensitive to their needs. Amen

4

Being special

Aim: To consider that we are all different and that makes us very special.

You will need: Five different flowers (for example, sunflower, gerbera, rose, anthurium and delphinium).

If possible, the flowers should be bought from a florist so that they are as varied and large as possible. The type of flowers used is unimportant, but the more different they are, the better. If flowers are not available, different teddy bears or different leaves could be used.

Assembly outline

Before the assembly, make sure that the flowers are out of sight. Explain that you have brought a few things to show during the assembly, but first you are going to give them some clues to what those things are. Explain that you are going to allow one child to make a guess after each clue. (Even if they guess the right answer very quickly, still read the remainder of the clues.)

- Clue 1: these things can't move on their own.
- Clue 2: these things are alive.
- Clue 3: these things can grow.
- Clue 4: all of them have some green on them.
- Clue 5: all of them are grown in soil.
- Clue 6: these things are often given to people to say 'thank you' or to show them that they are special or cared for.

Point out that these clues might suggest that the things you are going to show the children are very similar to each other, but in fact they are very different. Show the children the first flower—for example, the sunflower. Say how tall sunflowers can grow: the tallest recorded are over nine metres. Show the thickness of the stem, the arrangement of the petals, the colour and other details. Ask a child to come to the front to hold the sunflower.

Repeat this process for each flower, emphasising the details and the differences.

Explain that the five things you have shown the children are all flowers, so they have many things in common. However, each one is also completely different from the others. It is the differences that make the flowers interesting and unique. Point out that if there was only one type of flower, the world would be a much duller place in which to live. Ask the children to imagine a world where there was only one type of tree or one type of animal. Ask them to imagine what it would be like if there was only one shade of green and all the plants looked exactly the same.

Explain that sometimes we can look at other people and wish we were like them. We may look at someone who is a fast runner and wish we could be as fast as they are. We might wish we were cleverer or prettier, or made people laugh more easily, or had different hair or wore different clothes. However, we need to remember that it is the differences between us that make us unique and special.

Ask the children to imagine what it would be like if everyone in the world was good at running but couldn't do anything else, such as cooking, reading, riding a bike or counting. The world would not only be uninteresting, but we would also struggle to survive. Point out that each of us is different. We all look different, have different personalities and different talents, and will move on to get different jobs and do different things in the future. This is a wonderful thing!

Remind the children that each of them has many special characteristics that are unique to them. Some of these characteristics may not be as obvious as other people's are, but they are still as important. We may be good at making friends, caring for people or noticing when someone is feeling sad, or perhaps we have a smile that cheers everyone up. Just because our unique features are not immediately seen by everyone, it doesn't mean they are any less essential.

Remember: we are all different and that makes us even more special.

What the Bible says

Christians believe that God created a world full of variety and wonder. In **Genesis 1** we read that God made different plants, trees, birds, fish and animals. He didn't make just one kind—he made many! In **Genesis 1:31**, when the Bible describes the creation, it says, 'God saw all that he had made, and it was very good.'

Throughout the years, people have seen the beauty of creation and have described it in different ways. Many of the Psalms express the way people worshipped God when they saw the wonder of all he had made. **Psalm 8** is a great example of this: you may like to ask a child to read it out loud.

Christians also believe that, alongside the rest of creation, God made each of us special and different. In **Psalm 139:14**, the writer says, 'I praise you because I am fearfully and wonderfully made.'

Pause for thought

Are you happy with your gifts and talents? Do you sometimes wish that you could be like somebody else, who seems to be better than you at something? Take a moment to remind yourself that you are very special. There is no one else who is exactly the same as you in the entire world.

PRAYER
Dear God, thank you that each of us is different. Thank you that we all have characteristics, gifts and talents that make us unique. Please help us to be happy with who we are and to realise that each person is special. Amen

5

Celebrations

Aim: To consider that celebrations are happy times to share together.

You will need: Objects to represent two or three different celebrations (for example, Christmas, Easter, birthdays, Passover, Hanukkah or Eid).

Props could include:

- Christmas: artificial tree, decorations, present
- Easter: egg, hot cross bun
- Birthday: cake, present
- Passover: bread, wine
- Hanukkah: candles, other lights
- Eid: new clothes, present

Assembly outline

Place the props at the front of the room before the assembly begins and keep them covered until they are needed.

Ask for a volunteer to come forward. Uncover one set of props—for example, the Christmas tree and present.

Ask the volunteer to describe what Christmas morning is like in their home. Encourage the child to talk about the noise and excitement and any traditions they have. Invite the child to sit beside the tree with the present, and ask if it feels different sitting there alone than with all the usual Christmas excitement and noise around them. Ask which they prefer: they will probably say that they prefer their usual Christmas Day.

Invite another child to come forward and ask them what happens on their birthday. Encourage them to speak about their excitement when they open their presents, welcome visitors, go out for a meal or have a party. Ask the child to hold the birthday cake. Ask what they would feel like if they had to go and buy their own cake and if they had no one to sing to them or share the cake with them.

Adapt this outline for any of the other celebrations listed above, all of which involve people celebrating together.

Ask the children if they can think of other times when they may be involved in some kind of celebration. Examples could be a wedding, a christening, a time when someone has got a new job or passed exams, or being 'Star of the week' in school. Ask them to share some examples of these celebrations.

Explain that we all like to celebrate, whether it's a large event like a wedding or a surprise celebration for receiving an award in school, winning a sports competition or being offered a new job. Repeat some of the celebrations listed and ask if the children can spot what all of the situations have in common—that each celebration has other people present. We are unlikely to celebrate on our own; celebrations are no fun if we have no one to share them with. In fact, the most important thing about any celebration is not what present or prize we receive, but the people with whom we can share it.

What the Bible says

The Bible makes it clear that God loves people to celebrate. The book of Psalms is full of songs and poems that encourage us to look around and celebrate the wonder of the world and God's greatness. Here are a few examples:

- **Psalm 118:24** says, 'This day belongs to the Lord! Let's celebrate and be glad today' (CEV).
- **Psalm 98:4** says, 'Shout for joy to the Lord, all the earth, burst into jubilant song with music!'

God wants us to be happy, to celebrate and enjoy each other's company, but he also wants us to be sensitive to those who are around us.

In **Romans 12:15** it says, 'Rejoice with those who rejoice; mourn with those who mourn.'

When good things happen to the people around us, it is great to be happy with them. However, when sad things happen or our friends simply feel down in the dumps, then it is good to listen to them, be quiet with them and help them to move to a time when they can celebrate with us again.

Pause for thought

Close your eyes for a moment and think about a celebration that you have been involved in recently. It could be a wedding, a birthday party, a treat for an award at school or any other celebration. In your mind, picture the celebration and scan round the room to see the faces of the people who shared it with you. Think about each of the people you see in turn. In your mind, say their name and remember something special about that person. Remind yourself that the people in our lives are far more important than any of the gifts we ever receive.

PRAYER

Dear God, thank you for all the people who make our lives special. Thank you for times of celebration; thank you for treats and presents. Please help us to cherish our families and friends and all the people who work hard to make our lives special. Please help us to play our part in making them happy too. Amen

6

Choices we make

Aim: To consider the importance of making good decisions in our lives.

You will need: A small toy; a bar of chocolate; cards (or a screen) on which to write (or display) words.

Prepare cards with pairs of words that the children will have to choose between (one word per card). For example:

- Christmas — Easter
- football — cricket
- oranges — apples
- horses — rabbits
- art — science
- riding a bike — bouncing on a trampoline
- red — yellow
- chips — rice
- maths book — reading book

The exact pairs are not important as long as the children can make a choice between them. Use comparisons appropriate to the school and the age of the children.

Assembly outline

Ask the children if they have had to make any decisions this morning. Suggestions could be whether or not to get up as soon as their parent woke them; whether to have cereal or toast for breakfast; who to play with before school; whether to hold the door for someone as they came into school or to push in front of them. Point out that often we make decisions without even realising that we are doing it. Making choices is simply part of our everyday lives. However, there are times when we need to stop and think about the decisions that we are making.

Show the children the toy and the chocolate, and tell them that you want them to make a decision. Explain that they need to decide whether, given a choice, they would choose the toy or the chocolate as a present. Ask those who would choose the toy to raise their hands. Then ask those who would choose the chocolate to raise their hands.

Invite two people who made different choices to explain why they made their decision. Perhaps they chose the toy because they would enjoy playing with it, or the chocolate because they could share it with a friend. The reason doesn't matter, but point out that many factors can influence the choices that we make.

Explain that you want the children to make some more decisions. You are going to give them two choices and you want them to pick which one they prefer. It might be difficult to choose between the two but they must decide for one or the other.

For each pair of words, ask two volunteers to hold the cards at opposite sides of the room. If the numbers in the assembly are small, the children can all physically move to the appropriate side of the room to show their decision. If numbers are larger or space is restricted, the children should point to the side of the room that indicates their choice.

Show the children two cards—for example, 'oranges' and 'apples'. Ask them to point or move to the side of the room displaying their preferred fruit. Use words such as, 'Do you prefer apples or oranges? Given the choice, which would you choose? Point to the side of the room that shows your choice.' Repeat for each pair of cards.

If you are displaying the word pairs on a screen, ask the children to point to the side of the screen that shows their choice.

Admit that the decisions the children have just made are not very important. It doesn't matter if we prefer football or cricket, or enjoy riding our bike more than bouncing on a trampoline. In fact, it's great that we are all different and enjoy different things. However, many of the decisions that we make in our lives are more important. They affect not only ourselves but other people as well.

Ask the children for examples of choices they might make, which have an impact on other people. Many of our choices affect others. It may be the decision to say something unkind about a person, the decision not to let someone join in a game, the decision to be rude to a parent, the decision to mess around in class, or many more. The fact is that all of us have a big impact on the people around us.

Challenge the children to think about how their choices affect others. Encourage them to pause before they make a decision and consider how their choice will affect those around them.

What the Bible says

The Bible encourages us always to think about the needs of other people. Even more than this, it challenges us to put other people's needs above our own. **Philippians 2:3–4** says, 'Do nothing out of selfish ambition or vain conceit. Rather, in humility value others above yourselves, not looking to your own interests but each of you to the interests of others.'

There are many stories in the Gospels where Jesus is seen to think more about others than about himself. Even on the night before he died, he took the time to wash his disciples' feet. This was not a pleasant job, but Jesus wanted to do it to show the way in which we should put other people's needs ahead of our own. The story can be found in **John 13:1–15**.

Pause for thought

Pause for a moment and think about the choices that you have already made today. Have you made good choices? Think about the choices that you will need to make as you go through the day. Will you let people join in your games at break time? Will you help someone if they need help? Will you be polite and say 'thank you'? Will you stand up for someone if they are being picked on? Let's remember to stop and think before we make decisions.

PRAYER

Dear God, thank you for all the people who are part of our lives. Please help us to remember that the way we behave and the choices we make can affect those around us. Please help us to stop and think, and then make good decisions. Amen

7

Everyone is important

Aim: To consider that each person is important and that each person's actions affect other people.

You will need: A list of five general occupations (for example, teacher, doctor, farmer, refuse collector, fire fighter) or a list of five jobs in school (for example, cleaner, cook, teacher, head teacher, bursar).

Display the list of occupations at the front of the room. If you wish, ask people who carry out different jobs in school to attend the assembly and give a quick explanation of what their job entails.

Assembly outline

Ask a child to read the list of occupations (or jobs within school) displayed. Explain that you want all the children to think about the list and decide which occupation/job they consider to be the most important. Give the children a moment to think and then ask if any of them are willing to share their answer and their reason for making their choice.

When a child gives an answer, comment that it is a good answer but also ask an open question referring to a different occupation. For example, if a child states that being a doctor is the most important, agree that it is a good answer but then point out that the doctor may never have become a doctor if they had not been taught well at school by a teacher. If a child says that fire fighters are the most important because they save lives, ask if the fire fighters would be able to do their job effectively if they had nothing to eat, because the farmer had not grown any food. The idea is to help the children to see the essential nature of each occupation.

Work through each occupation in turn, pointing out how essential each one is and how it affects our lives. Without teachers, we would be unable to learn to read and write, which would affect us greatly in our futures. Without doctors, we may become sick and be unable to get the help we need to get better. Without farmers, we may not have the food we need to keep alive and healthy. Without refuse collectors, our world would be dirty, smelly and unhygienic, and we could become ill. Without emergency services, we would not be rescued in fires or car accidents, so our world would not be as safe a place to live in.

Alternatively, talk through each job carried out in school in the same way, pointing out its importance. If people did not clean our school, it would be dirty and an unpleasant place to be. If no one cooked our school dinners, we would all be hungry. If there were no teachers, we would not be able to learn, and school wouldn't be as much fun. If there was no bursar, many activities in school would not be organised.

Explain that all of us might be asked to carry out different jobs in school or at home. It may be making a bed, tidying up, looking after a new child, collecting the register, putting away the playground equipment, buying something from a shop or looking after a younger brother or sister. Some of these things may seem like very small responsibilities and may not appear to be very important. However, every job we do and every task we take part in will affect other people in some way.

Point out that everyone has different abilities and skills. In the future, all the children will have different jobs and different roles in life. However, we all need to remember that every person is important and has something special to give to the world.

What the Bible says

1 Corinthians 12:12–20 describes people as being like the parts of a body. It says how silly it would be for a foot to start complaining that it isn't a hand and refusing to do the job of being a foot. If one part of the body isn't working properly, it has a big effect on the rest of the body. In the same way, each person has a special role to play in the world or in a school or in the home. Each person is vitally important.

Pause for thought

Think for a moment about your family. What do they do that affects your life in some way? Maybe your parent or carer goes out to work so that you have enough money to buy things. Maybe they cook your dinner, make your bed, take you on trips, read you a story at night and tuck you into bed. Each of these things is important to you; each of these things matters.

Think about your friends. What do they do that affects your life in some way? Maybe they let you play with their toys, invite you to sleepovers, play games with you at break time and come to your parties. All of these things are important, as they make you feel loved and special.

Now take a moment to think about yourself. Everything you do and say affects other people in some way. Let's make a special effort today to realise that we are important in the world and what we do really does matter.

PRAYER

Dear God, thank you for all the people who are important in our lives. Please remind us that each person is special. Help us to behave in a way that is good for those around us, as we learn to play our part in making the world a better place. Amen

8

Friendship

Aim: To consider that one of the greatest gifts in the world is friendship.

You will need: 30 old greetings cards, cut in half; another card, also cut in half, but with one of the halves discarded; two volunteers.

Use a mixture of cards—Christmas, birthday, anniversary and so on.

If you want more than two volunteers to join in, increase the number of cards accordingly (10–15 cards per person). Ensure that one of your cards does *not* have two matching halves.

Assembly outline

Show the children one of the cards that has been cut in half but can be put together to make a whole. Ask for two volunteers who are good at jigsaw puzzles, and invite them to come to the front. Tell them that you have lots of cards that have been cut in half and muddled up. You are going to spread out the pieces of card and, when you say 'go', you want the volunteers to unmuddle them for you.

Explain that each volunteer can only hold one piece of card in their hand until they see the matching half. They can then pick up the matching half and place the pair in a specific area (for example, at the side of the room). If they spot a matching pair while holding a different card, they may place the card they are holding on the floor and pick up the matching ones.

(Make sure the volunteers are each given 'storage' areas at equal distances from the muddled cards: they will complain if it is not fair.)

Ask the volunteers to turn away while you spread the cards face up on the floor. You may like to divide the remaining children into two or more teams so that they can cheer for the different volunteers. Count down from ten to build up the atmosphere and when you say 'go' the game can begin.

The volunteers pick up a card from the floor, find its matching half, place the complete card in their designated area and repeat the process until all the cards are complete.

Remember that one card does not have a match. If a child picks this card up and cannot find the other half, allow them to search for a while and then suggest that they try another card. (The volunteers will probably be quite indignant when they discover that one of the cards did not have a match, especially if they spent a lot of time looking for it.)

At the end, let the volunteers sit down but leave the unmatched card on the floor. Ask the children to imagine that the card left on the floor has feelings. What do they think the card feels like, all alone in the middle of the floor? Point out that the volunteers chose one card at a time, searched around and found a match for each one, but this card didn't fit in with any of the other cards. When the volunteers had a card in their hand, they looked at this card but never chose it as a match. A couple of times it was picked up, but, when it wouldn't fit with any other card, it was simply dropped back on to the floor.

Explain that some of us have good friends. We 'fit in' with them. Maybe we have matching hobbies or matching characters; we find the same things funny and we enjoy the same things. However, some people don't have a friend like that. They feel on their own, as if they don't fit in. They feel different and left out.

Having friends is a wonderful thing but we should always be careful that we don't push other people out. We should always try to look for people who are on their own and need a friend. Having friends is a wonderful gift.

What the Bible says

King Solomon is a famous biblical king who was well known for his wisdom. He wrote down many wise sayings, which are recorded for us in the Bible, in the books of Proverbs and Ecclesiastes. A famous saying from **Proverbs 17:17** is 'A friend loves at all times.'

Sometimes friends make us sad and let us down. Sometimes we do the same to them. However, a real friend will always try to understand us and will love and forgive us when we get things wrong. In **Ecclesiastes 4:9–10**, Solomon writes, 'Two are better than one… If either of them falls down, one can help the other up.' This reminds us that true friends support each other. They are always there to help each other in times of difficulty.

Pause for thought

How important are your friends to you? Do you ever show your friends that you care about them? Do you know children who are always on their own and don't have any friends? How do you think they feel about that? Could you do something today to help them to make friends and feel less lonely?

PRAYER

Dear God, thank you for all our friends. Thank you especially for ...... [ask the children to think of a particular friend as they pray]. Please help us to be good friends. Help us to act in unselfish ways and always be ready to listen and try to understand. Please help us to watch out for others who are feeling lonely. Help us to know how to include them and help us not to give up trying. Amen

q

Giving to others

Aim: To consider that what we give out to others often has a big effect on us too.

This assembly works well in the context of making visitors to the school feel welcome, and events involving the elderly, such as Grandparents' Day.

You will need: A boomerang (or a boomerang shape cut out of card); a hula hoop; a prearranged volunteer to copy your facial expressions.

As it will be impossible to throw a boomerang effectively indoors, you may wish to download a video clip of how to throw it, so the children can see that it returns to the thrower.

With the hula hoop, you need to be able to spin it forward in such a way that it returns to you. If necessary, find someone else who is prepared to demonstrate this trick.

Assembly outline

Show the children the boomerang and ask if anyone knows what it is called and what it does. If required, show the video of how a boomerang is thrown. Explain that, although it takes a lot of practice to do it correctly, a boomerang will turn back on itself and come back to the thrower.

Show the children the hula hoop. Ask if anyone can keep the hoop spinning on their waist for a long time, and invite someone to the front to demonstrate. You may like to have a number of hoops available and see which child can keep it going the longest. Ask if anyone can do any different tricks with the hoop. Be prepared for children to skip with them, spin them on their arms or jump through them. You are looking for a child who can spin the hoop forward in such a way that it reverses itself and comes back to them, rather like a boomerang. If none of the children can do this, either demonstrate it yourself or ask someone else to do so.

Once the children have been shown how to make the hoop return to them, ask a few to come forward to try.

Explain that, in some ways, the boomerang and the hoop are similar to the actions that we take in our lives. The way we behave, the way we treat other people and the things we say can have a big effect not just on others but also on ourselves. For example, if we are unkind to others, they are much less likely to want to be our friends; if we always want to play our own games and never share, children are unlikely to want to play with us; if we say mean things or hurt other children, people will keep away from us.

However, the opposite is also true. If we are kind to others, they will want to be our friends; if we are friendly and sharing, people will want to play with us.

Ask the prearranged volunteer to come forward. Ask the other children to watch carefully and spot what is happening. Tell them that you are feeling sad, and pretend to cry. The volunteer should look at you and begin to cry too. Now show a variety of facial expressions or actions, giving time for the volunteer to copy each one in turn. Actions could include pulling a grumpy face, laughing, dancing, stamping your feet crossly and smiling.

Ask the children what they have just seen the volunteer do. Explain that, just as the emotions you were feeling were passed on to the volunteer, so the signals that we give out to others are passed on and affect the way other people feel and behave. The best example of this is probably a smile. If we smile at someone, they will usually smile back. Sometimes, just smiling at someone can change their day from a sad one, in which they feel as if no one cares about them, to a happy one, in which they feel cared for and loved. Point out that many elderly people live alone and have little contact with the outside world. A smile can make a big difference to them.

Challenge the children to think about what they 'give out' to others, through the things they do and the emotions or expressions that they share. Encourage them to treat others in the way that they would like to be treated, and always to remember that they can share happiness simply with a smile.

What the Bible says

In the Gospel of Matthew there is a section known as the Sermon on the Mount (**Matthew 5—7**), where Jesus teaches us some very important things. For example, in **Matthew 5:44**, Jesus tells us that we should love our enemies. In

Matthew 7:1–5 we read that we should be very careful when making judgements about other people; instead we should realise that none of us is perfect. In **Matthew 7:12** Jesus says, 'In everything, do to others what you would have them do to you.' This makes it clear that we should treat other people in the same way that we would like them to treat us, and that's quite a challenge.

Pause for thought

How do you like to be treated? Do you like it when people shout at you? Do you like it when people are rude to you or leave you out of their games? How do you feel when someone is kind to you? Can you think of a time when you were sad and someone cared for you, or you fell over and someone helped you up, or you were struggling with your work and someone took the time to help? How did this make you feel?

Remember that the things you do make a difference to others. Let's always try to give out things that we would like to come back to us.

PRAYER

Dear God, please help us to treat other people in the way that we would like to be treated. Help us to think about how our actions make others feel. Please remind us that even a smile can make a difference and can brighten up someone's day. Amen

10

Healthy eating

Aim: To consider the importance of eating a balanced healthy diet.

You will need:

- A kettle; a mug, a tea bag; a banana; a building brick
- A large toy car or picture of a car; a bottle of lemonade; a bottle of milk
- A selection of foods or pictures of food that contribute to a balanced diet
- Two cards, one showing the word 'often' and one showing the word 'occasionally'
- A set of balance scales; small blocks
- The words 'carbohydrate', 'protein', 'fats', 'vitamins', 'minerals' and 'water' on cards or on a screen (optional, depending on the age groups present)

The banana and brick are simply illustrations of things that will not make a kettle work. They can be replaced by any items of your choice.

Similarly, the lemonade and milk are simply illustrations of things that will not make a car work properly, so they can be replaced by other liquids.

The foods will be used as part of a game considering how often they should be eaten. Choose examples to fit into the categories of 'often' and 'occasionally'.

Assembly outline

Pretend that you have been in a rush this morning and haven't yet had time to make a drink. Explain that, as you are thirsty, you are going to make a cup of tea. (You will not actually be doing this, so there are no safety issues.) Make a show of picking up the tea bag and placing it in the mug. Point out that you have already put water in the kettle so it's ready to boil. Look round for somewhere to plug it in, then pick up the banana and pretend to plug it into that. When the children laugh, ask them why they are laughing and pretend to plug the kettle into the brick instead.

Ask the children why it is silly to plug the kettle into either of these objects. They will agree that the only way the kettle will work properly is if electricity is passed into it.

Show the children the toy car. Ask a volunteer to describe what happens at a filling station. Pick up the lemonade and milk and ask what would happen if, instead of filling the car with petrol or diesel, you used these liquids instead. Explain that, just as the kettle will not work without electricity, the car will work properly only if we put the correct liquid into it. Say that the same is true for our bodies. Our bodies will only work well if we put the right things into them.

Show the children the set of balance scales. Place five blocks in one pan and ask a volunteer to come forward to make the scales balance. Explain that, to keep our bodies healthy, we need to 'balance' the foods that we take into them. If we eat just chips and biscuits all the time, we will not be healthy. However, if we eat just lettuce and apples all the time, we will not be healthy either. We need a balance of lots of different kinds of food.

Ask the children to suggest foods that will keep them healthy. Most children will say 'fruit and vegetables' but make it clear that most foods are good in small amounts.

Depending on the age of the children present, show the food or pictures of food, or the cards with 'carbohydrate', 'protein', 'fats', 'vitamins', 'minerals' and 'water' written on them. Explain that, if we are to be healthy, we need to eat foods from each of these categories.

Ask for two volunteers to hold the 'often' and 'occasionally' cards at the front of the room. Show the remaining children one of the food items or pictures of food, and ask if they think the food should be eaten often or just occasionally. After a brief discussion, ask a volunteer to come forward and hold the food next to the appropriate sign. Repeat this for each food item or picture.

Remind the children that, just like the car, our bodies work best when we put the right food into them.

What the Bible says

The Bible tells us that God made the world and everything in it. It tells us that God intended us to use the things he created, for food. In **Genesis 1:29** we read, 'Then God said, "I give you every seed-bearing plant on the face of the whole earth and every tree that has fruit with seed in it. They will be yours for food."' Later, in **Genesis 9:3**, God says, 'Everything that lives and moves about will be food for you. Just as I gave you the green plants, I now give you everything.'

The Bible also talks about the importance of looking after our bodies. **1 Corinthians 6:19** describes our body as being like a temple where God lives; this means that it is very important to look after it.

Pause for thought

Many people in this world do not have enough food to eat each day. Think for a moment about how fortunate we are to have so many foods to choose from. Think about your own body. Each of us has an amazing body that helps us move, breathe, have fun and enjoy life. Let's remember to look after our bodies and to treat them in a way that recognises how precious they are.

PRAYER
Dear God, thank you for our bodies. Thank you for the amazing choice of foods available to us. Please help us to take care of our bodies by eating a balanced diet so that we can grow strong and healthy. Amen

Healthy exercise

Aim: To consider the importance of exercise as part of a healthy lifestyle.

You will need: A pile of paper; pens; a collection of PE equipment, such as hoops, balls and beanbags.

You can use plain A4 paper, but it makes for an attractive display if the paper is cut in different shapes—for example, racket or ball shapes.

If possible, ask some children who enjoy different forms of exercise outside school to be prepared to demonstrate their skills during the assembly. For example, they could perform a short ballet dance, show some judo moves, do some cheerleading or show how to hold a golf club correctly.

Assembly outline

Ask the children if they can think of any sports or types of exercise. You may like to give them 30 seconds to speak to the people on either side of them to see how many different sports they can come up with.

Invite the children to put their hands up to name just one type of sport or exercise. As they name a different sport, ask them to come to the front and write the sport in large letters on a piece of paper and hold it up for everyone to see. (You might need an adult or older child to help younger children with their spelling.)

At first there will be lots of hands up as the more well-known sports are named, but it will soon become more difficult. Eventually there will be a lot of children standing at the front. Point out that there is an amazing choice of sports and exercises that we can do, which means that there is something that everyone can enjoy.

Mention that many of the sports written on the papers are team games, such as football, netball and cricket. Some people don't like to play these sports as they think other people are much better players than they are. Sometimes, people don't want to take part in sport because they feel as if they always lose, or they don't like being competitive.

Feeling like this can stop people from getting involved in any sport. However, exercise is not about being competitive; it is about keeping the body healthy. Explain that exercise can take place in the playground, in our own homes and in a wide variety of other places.

Show the collection of PE equipment. Ask the children to use their imaginations and come forward to demonstrate three different games or types of exercise that can be carried out using this equipment. For example, the hoop can be spun round the waist, it can be rolled forward, with the child chasing it, or it can be used for skipping. A beanbag can be thrown in the air and caught or it can be balanced on the head while the child walks quickly. A few beanbags can be placed on the floor so that the children can do shuttle runs to collect them. Point out that all these uses are forms of exercise.

You may want to challenge the children to see who can make up the most original, easy-to-play game using the equipment. The winning game could be taught to all the other children later in the week.

Explain that exercising regularly has many benefits. It helps us develop strong, healthy muscles, joints and bones, and it keeps our hearts healthy. It also helps us maintain a sensible weight, sleep well, get on with other people and concentrate well, so it makes us feel much happier.

Research shows that children who do lots of exercise are likely to carry on exercising as they get older. However, children who don't exercise much are less likely to start doing so when they become adults. This means that the choices we make as children may well determine how fit we are in the future.

Challenge the children to think about how much exercise they do. Make the point that even walking round the playground a few times during break, walking to school or playing outside instead of watching TV can make a massive difference to their health. Remind them that exercise can be enjoyed by everyone, irrespective of how talented they are.

You may want to use this opportunity to introduce the children to a Sports Week or a special sports event. If possible, use this to encourage them to try something new: it could be the start of a lifelong hobby.

What the Bible says

The Bible tells us that everybody is different and that this makes us all very special. Christians believe that God not only made each person, but that he knew them even before they were born. In **Jeremiah 1:5** we read, 'Before I formed you in the womb I knew you.' Whatever our talents may be, they are a gift from God.

The Bible also encourages us to be happy for other people and to recognise their value. **Romans 12:15** says, 'Rejoice with those who rejoice,' and **Philippians 2:3** says, 'Do nothing out of selfish ambition or vain conceit. Rather, in humility value others above yourselves.' It is important to try to celebrate with others and not to let feelings of jealousy get in the way.

The Bible describes our bodies as 'temples' where God's Spirit lives (**1 Corinthians 6:19**). Because of this, Christians believe that they should do their best to keep their bodies healthy.

Pause for thought

Do you enjoy taking part in sport? Have you given up playing something because you feel that you are not very good or because someone has made an unkind comment or even laughed at you? Take a moment to realise that the main purpose of sport is enjoyment. Is there something you would really like to try, but you have been too frightened? Make a decision to have a go! Make a decision to try something new: it may be the activity that you do for the rest of your life.

PRAYER

Dear God, thank you for our amazing bodies. Thank you for the physical activities we can do. Please help us to look after our bodies by eating healthily, exercising regularly and sleeping well. Amen

12

Healthy sleeping

Aim: To consider the importance of sleep if we are to stay healthy.

You will need:

- The following words and numbers written on separate cards: human baby, human adult, human elderly, 16 hours, 8 hours, 6 hours
- The following animals and numbers written on separate cards: tiger, pig, giraffe, bat, duck, hamster, 2 hours, 8 hours, 11 hours, 14 hours, 16 hours, 20 hours
- Pillow, duvet and mat (optional)

Assembly outline

Explain that you have brought something to the assembly to give the children a clue to what you are going to be thinking about. Show them the pillow and duvet; you may want to have a mat ready so that you can lie down and pretend to go to sleep.

Ask how many of the children like going to bed at night and how many of them would rather stay up late. Ask if they think it is important to go to sleep, and their reasons for giving their answer.

Invite three volunteers to come to the front and give each one a card to hold, showing the words 'human baby', 'human adult' and 'human elderly'. Ask the children if they think a baby, adult or elderly person would need more sleep and why. You may want to discuss which age bracket would be the most active, which would be growing the most, which would be working the longest hours and which would be likely to relax more.

Ask three further volunteers to hold up the signs for 16, 8 and 6 hours. Explain that the cards refer to the average amount of sleep needed by babies, adults and elderly people. Ask the children to guess which number goes with each age bracket. (The answers are: human baby, 16 hours; human adult, 8 hours; and human elderly, 6 hours.) Allow the volunteers to sit down.

Explain that it is not only adults who need their sleep. Animals also need varying amounts of sleep. Invite six volunteers to hold up the cards with the animal names written on them. Ask a further six volunteers to hold up the 2, 8, 11, 14, 16 and 20 hour signs. Explain that the numbers of hours on the cards show the average length of sleep time per day/night for the animals written on the other cards. Point out what a wide range of sleeping times animals have, and ask the children what they think might affect the amount of time an animal spends sleeping. Suggestions could be the size of the animal, how active the animal is, whether the animal is nocturnal, and so on. Ask a pair of children to come to the front to match the animals with the number of hours spent sleeping, or take a vote from all the children.

Some of the answers will surprise the children: giraffe, 2 hours; pig, 8 hours; duck, 11 hours; hamster, 14 hours; tiger, 16 hours; bat, 20 hours.

Ask the children why they think it is necessary that we go to sleep. Explain that much of our growth occurs while we sleep and that our bodies need time to rest so that they can be refreshed for all the activities of the following day. Scientists have carried out investigations which show that a lot of brain development happens while we are asleep. Lack of sleep has been shown to make people grumpier, hungrier, less able to concentrate, more forgetful and more likely to make poor decisions. It can stop people from carrying out even simple tasks as well as they would if they were properly rested.

Point out that children often love to stay up late. As a special treat, there is nothing wrong with this, but, if we always have late nights and never catch up on our sleep, it will affect our behaviour. A lack of sleep can make children less able to concentrate in school, which can have a long-term effect on their education. In fact, scientists say that getting enough sleep is as important as eating healthily and taking regular exercise. If this assembly is being used in conjunction with the healthy eating and healthy exercise assemblies, reinforce the point that all three things are needed for a healthy lifestyle.

What the Bible says

There are many times recorded in the Bible when Jesus went off alone to have some peace and to pray. In **Matthew**

8:23–27 and **Mark 4:35–41** we read a story about Jesus and his disciples being caught in a terrible storm on the Sea of Galilee. Despite the fact that the wind was howling and the waves were pouring over the sides of their boat, Jesus was peacefully sleeping.

Psalm 4:8 also tells us that we can sleep in peace because God is watching over us.

Pause for thought

What do you do at bedtime when you are asked to go to sleep? Next time you complain, remember that while you sleep, your body is doing all sorts of amazing things that will prepare you for getting the most out of the following day.

PRAYER

Dear God, thank you for our amazing bodies. Please help us to do everything we can to keep them healthy. Thank you that we have homes in which we can sleep peacefully. Please be with all those people in the world who have nowhere to sleep and no homes to go to. Amen

13

It's not fair!

Aim: To consider that sometimes things are not fair, but, when they're not, we have a choice to make: we can complain and moan or we can realise that it really doesn't matter.

You will need: Beanbags or balls of different sizes; two cones; different sized containers (for example, bucket, large box, small box, plant pot and bowl); blindfold (optional); a teacher to keep score.

Assembly outline

Ask for four volunteers and explain that they are going to form two teams with two people in each. (Team 2 are going to have a number of unfair disadvantages, so choose children who will be able to cope with this situation. You may even want to prime them before the assembly and ask them to stay cheerful and not complain.)

Draw an imaginary line up the centre of the room to divide the remaining children into two groups of supporters. Allocate a side of the room to each team.

Explain that you are going to give the teams a challenge, and that they will receive points which will be added up to find the winning team. Position the cones to mark where each team will stand and ask the teams to line up behind them. Place a bucket a sensible distance away from each cone. Say that the teams are going to have a chance to practise before the competition begins. Give each child a beanbag or ball and ask them to take turns in throwing them into the bucket.

Once the children have practised, announce that the competition is about to begin. The children will win a point for their team every time they get a beanbag in the container. Invite Team 1 to take one throw each, but, before they do, move their cone nearer to the bucket so that it is much easier for them to score points. Ask Team 2 to take their turn, but, before they do, move their cone further away so that it is more difficult.

Someone in the audience or one of the team members will complain. When they do, move both cones back to their original positions and ask if everyone is happy now. Invite Team 1 to take another throw, but, before they do, replace the bucket with the large box, so that it is easier to score points. When Team 2 take their throw, replace the bucket with a plant pot to make it more difficult.

Repeat the procedure a few times, each time making the task easier for Team 1 and more difficult for Team 2. Suggestions for making the task more difficult could include increasing the distance, reducing the size of container, blindfolding Team 2, making Team 2 stand on one leg to throw, and so on. If people complain during the game, just smile and tell them not to worry, or smile and move the equipment around.

When the competition is over (make it as long or short as you want), ask the scorer to add up the scores. Try to build up the atmosphere before announcing that Team 1 are the winners. Because of the unfairness of the competition, Team 1 should have a far higher score than Team 2. If not, feel free to add extra points on to Team 1's score, as the whole point of the exercise is that it isn't fair.

Ask the children what they thought about the competition. Ask them if they thought Team 1 should have won and why/why not. It is likely that some of the children will be quite indignant.

Explain that you made the competition unfair on purpose. You agree that it was easier for Team 1 and that the result was biased. However, in our lives we are constantly coming up against situations that are unfair. Ask the children to think of examples of things that they feel are unfair. Be aware that there could be a wide range of answers.

Say that when we come up against things that we feel are unfair, we are faced with a choice. We can moan and complain, we can just keep going, or we can try to do something about the situation. Point out that our attitudes make a big difference. Sometimes, when something is not fair, it is good to try to sort it out. For example, if we see someone being bullied, it is a good idea to go and tell someone about it, as the treatment is unfair and should be put right.

However, there are times when things seem unfair and we can't do anything about them. For example, it may seem unfair that someone else is good at sport and reading, when we struggle with both. In this case, we still have a choice:

we can accept that people are all different and we all have different gifts and abilities, or we can be jealous and try to make things unpleasant for the person concerned. Another example may be when a child in school is given a special prize or privilege that we don't have. In this situation it might be appropriate to go and talk about our concerns with a teacher, but simply moaning and complaining will not achieve anything.

Challenge the children to pause and think about the way they react when they think something is unfair today.

What the Bible says

The Bible encourages us to look for the positive things in any situation. In **Philippians 4:8** it says, 'Whatever is true, whatever is noble, whatever is right, whatever is pure, whatever is lovely, whatever is admirable—if anything is excellent or praiseworthy—think about such things.' This means that even when life seems very unfair, we can still look for something positive. The Bible also encourages us not to moan and complain. **Philippians 2:14** says, 'Do everything without grumbling and arguing.'

Pause for thought

What do you do when things go wrong or seem unfair? Can you think of a situation recently when you were complaining and moaning? What would have been a better attitude to adopt? Next time you feel that a situation is unfair, why not pause for a moment and decide what the best attitude and the best course of action would be?

PRAYER

Dear God, thank you that you know us well and you understand that sometimes we feel as if things are not fair. Please help us to know when we should speak out against unfairness and when we should keep silent. Please help us to treat others fairly and to see how important each person's needs are. Amen

14

Journey of life

Aim: To encourage the children to consider life as a journey during which they should grasp every opportunity to try new things and meet new people.

This theme works well as a transition assembly—for example, for school leavers.

You will need: Pictures of lots of different modes of transport (for example, car, bus, bicycle, electric scooter); spare paper or cards; pictures of unusual modes of transport from other countries (optional).

If pictures of modes of transport are not available, write the words on cards instead. It is good to include a couple of unusual ideas, such as a skateboard, rowing boat or hot-air balloon.

Assembly outline

Explain to the children that you want to find out how they all travelled to school this morning. Invite them all to stand up, and then to sit down when you name the transport they used for their journey. First, ask them to sit down if they came to school by car, then if they came by bus, then by bike, then if they walked (using their legs as a mode of transport). If any children are still standing, ask them how they travelled to school.

Ask the children if they have ever been on holiday, and encourage them to think about how they travelled to their destination. Explain that when you were preparing this assembly, you found pictures of lots of different forms of transport. Ask the children to name any mode of transport. If a child names one that you have a picture of, invite them to come to the front and hold that picture so that everyone can see it. If they think of an unusual idea, invite them to write the name of that mode of transport (or draw a picture of it) on a spare piece of paper or card, and hold it up.

Display the pictures of unusual forms of transport from other countries, if available.

Ask the children what preparation might be needed before embarking on a long journey, to make it a pleasant experience. Examples could be booking a ticket, making sure the car is in good working order, preparing a picnic, finding entertainment for the journey, booking a place to stay en route, buying a map or setting the satnav.

Say that sometimes our lives are described as journeys. We all have a starting point and an ending point. We can't determine when we are born or when we die, but we can know that our journey through life will be a wonderful, exciting experience.

When we set off on a long journey, we often feel excited about what lies ahead. We imagine that we are going to visit unknown places and meet new people. We expect to have experiences that we have never had before and to try new things. If we went on holiday and never tried any of the new experiences open to us, we could miss out on many things that we might have enjoyed or learnt.

Ask the children if they can describe any new experience that they have enjoyed while on holiday. It could be a new food, a new activity, making new friends and so on.

Explain that during our life journeys we need to make the most of every opportunity that comes our way. If, for instance, we get the chance to meet new people, try new sports, learn something different or visit new places, we should always make the most of the opportunities. We may try something and find that we don't enjoy it, but if we don't try, we will never know if we have missed out on something amazing.

If the assembly is being used as a transition assembly, explain that, as the children move into a new school, they will have many amazing opportunities. Encourage them to make the most of these opportunities and never to be afraid to have a go. Remind them that they might try something new that will be the activity they enjoy doing most in their lives. New experiences can be life-changing.

What the Bible says

The Bible tells us about twelve of Jesus' special friends, or disciples. Before they followed Jesus, these men had many different occupations, including tax collecting and fishing. When Jesus asked them to join him on his travels, it must have seemed to them like a frightening new journey to set out on. However, the disciples saw amazing miracles and their lives were totally changed.

Often in the Bible, when people try something new or set off on a different pathway, God reminds them that he will be with them wherever they go. In **Joshua 1:9**, when Joshua was about to take on a scary new role as the leader of the Israelites, God said, 'Do not be afraid; do not be discouraged, for the Lord your God will be with you wherever you go.'

Pause for thought

Think about something that you especially enjoy doing. It may be riding your bike, reading, making models, sewing or swimming. Imagine if you had never been willing to have a go at that particular activity. You would never have experienced the fun, excitement and enjoyment that you now find the activity brings. Remember that you never know how much you will enjoy something until you try it. Always take the opportunities that come your way.

PRAYER
Dear God, thank you for all the new opportunities that we are given in our lives. Please help us never to be afraid of trying something new. Help us to move through our journey of life with joy and excitement, caring for other people on the way. Amen

15

Kindness

Aim: To consider that kindness may cost little but can make a massive difference to someone's life.

You will need: Eight chairs; clothes for dressing up as an old person; heavy carrier bags; a bunch of flowers; the following five sentences written on pieces of paper:

- I have no one to play with.
- I don't feel very well.
- My dog is sick and I feel sad.
- I am tired.
- I have so much to do.

Before the assembly, rehearse the following simple sketch, which you will describe as it takes place.

Set out eight chairs as if they were seats on a bus. Eight children board the bus, sit on the chairs and talk to each other in loud voices. You will ask the audience how they think the children are feeling.

A child dressed as an old person carrying heavy bags climbs on to the bus, looking worried and tired. You will ask the audience how they think the old person is feeling.

All of the children on the bus look at the old person and stop talking for a moment before seven of them turn away and continue to talk. The eighth child looks at the old person and then stands up to let him or her sit down. The old person gives a huge sigh, smiles, says 'thank you' and sits down. The other seven children stop talking and look at the standing child. You will ask the audience how the old person, eighth child and seven other children are now feeling.

A prearranged act of kindness will also take place during the assembly. A child might give a bunch of flowers to an unsuspecting member of staff for something that they do on a regular basis—for example, running an after-school club or just smiling all the time. Make sure the child says 'thank you' in a loud voice so that everyone can hear.

Assembly outline

Ask the children how they are feeling today. Invite them to put up their hands if they are feeling happy, sad, excited, worried and so on. Explain that some children are going to perform a short sketch and you are going to stop them occasionally during the sketch to ask the audience what the people in the sketch are feeling. Perform the sketch as suggested above, asking the children to identify the feelings. Once the sketch has finished, ask the children why Child 8 stood up. Ask if they thought it was the right thing to do. Ask if anyone can come up with words to describe Child 8's action.

Point out that Child 8 did something kind. This child was not just thinking about themselves, but was thinking about other people. Explain that it would have been very easy for Child 8 to pretend that they hadn't noticed the old person. It would have been easy to ignore the situation and continue to talk to their friends. But Child 8 chose to be kind. Being kind to others is a choice that we can all make.

Ask for a volunteer to hold up the first sentence written on paper. Give a brief explanation, such as, 'Today this child is feeling a bit sad because his two best friends are off school sick and he has no one to play with.' Ask the children, 'What would you do?'

Repeat with each of the five sentences. You may want to relate the last two questions to a parent at home or teacher in school. Make sure the question 'What would you do?' is asked each time.

Explain that all of us have the choice whether to be kind or not. We all find ourselves in situations every day when we can choose to help or not to help; to think about other people or to think about ourselves; to be kind or to be unkind. However, sometimes we can be kind without being placed in a specific situation: we can choose to be kind simply to make someone feel good. Call out the prearranged child volunteer to give the flowers to a staff member.

Explain that a spontaneous act of kindness can bring a lot of happiness to someone. It might be simply saying 'thank you' for something that we usually take for granted (like having our dinner made for us) or saying something encouraging to a friend.

You may want to use this assembly to introduce a 'Kindness Week challenge', in which each child is challenged to carry out an act of kindness every day.

What the Bible says

The Bible has a lot to say about thinking of other people and being kind. In **Luke 10:25–37**, Jesus tells the story of the good Samaritan. In this story, an unlikely person stops to help a man who has been hurt and robbed. Jesus says that we should always love and care for other people. You may like to retell the story of the good Samaritan as part of the assembly.

Ephesians 4:32 says, 'Be kind and compassionate to one another.'

Pause for thought

Can you think of a time when someone was kind to you? Think about how you felt when that person was kind. Can you think of a time when you were kind to someone else? How did that make you feel? Today we will all have to choose whether we want to be kind or whether we want to simply think about ourselves. What choice are you going to make? Can you think of something kind that you could do today?

PRAYER

Dear God, thank you that you always care about us. Thank you for people who are kind to us and make us feel happy and loved. Please help us always to think about other people and to show them that we care, by our actions. Amen

16

Keeping promises

Aim: To consider the importance of keeping a promise.

You will need: A box containing promises written on pieces of paper; two pieces of card, one showing the word 'Easy' and the other showing the word 'Difficult', in large letters; a box containing the biblical promises from 'What the Bible says' (optional).

The promises in the box should be at different levels of difficulty/seriousness. For example:

- I promise to keep my room tidy.
- I promise never to shout at my brother or sister again.
- I promise to do my best.
- I promise to be your friend for ever.
- The court of law promise: 'I promise before Almighty God that the evidence which I shall give shall be the truth, the whole truth, and nothing but the truth.'
- The Monarch's coronation promise (made after the reading of a list of actions regarding governing countries, upholding laws and following God): 'The

things which I have here before promised, I will perform and keep. So help me God.'

You may want to include promises specific to children within the school.

Assembly outline

In preparation, display the 'Easy' and 'Difficult' cards at opposite sides of the room.

Ask the children what they think a 'promise' is. Can they think of any promises that they have made or that have been made to them? Invite some children to share these promises with everyone else.

Ask if any of the children have ever gone back on a promise or ever had anyone break a promise that was made to them. Explain that some promises we make are easier to keep than others. (Point out that there are occasions when we make a promise that we fully intend to keep, but something happens which means that it is impossible to do so.)

Invite a child to come forward to pick a card from the box and read it out loud. If necessary, explain what the promise refers to (for example, the coronation or court of law promise). Ask the children if they think the promise would be difficult to keep, and if they think it is an important one to keep. After the discussion, ask them to raise their hands to vote on whether the promise would be easy or difficult to keep. Place the card next to the 'Easy' or 'Difficult' sign, dependent on the outcome of the vote.

Repeat this process for each card in the box.

Ask the children how they feel when promises are broken. Explain that it matters when we break promises to other people. It can make people sad. It can also make them feel that we can't be trusted.

Encourage the children to stop and think before they make any promises. Suggest that it is better not to say anything than to make a promise that we know we can't or won't keep.

Ask the question, 'Is it ever right to break a promise?' After listening to the children's answers, point out that occasionally someone might ask us to promise something that we feel scared or worried about. For example, they might hurt us or one of our friends in some way and make us promise to keep it a secret. Make it clear that if this ever happens, it is absolutely right to tell someone whom they trust about it.

What the Bible says

The Bible tells us that God always keeps his promises. Here are a few of the promises that God has made.

- God will always be with you (**Joshua 1:9**).
- No matter what happens, God will never stop loving you (**Romans 8:38–39**).
- God has a good plan for your life (**Jeremiah 32:40**).

You may want to place these promises in a box and ask the children to pull them out to read them, or ask the children to read the verses from a Bible.

Pause for thought

Have you ever made a promise to someone? It could be something like 'I'll play with you at break time' or 'I'll sit with you on the bus.' Think for a moment about how the other person will feel if you break this promise. They will feel let down and sad. Remember that it is better not to make a promise than to make one that you don't intend to keep. Let's make a decision to be people who can be trusted to keep our promises and always do the things that we say.

PRAYER

Dear God, thank you for the promises that you make to love us and care for us. Sometimes we find it hard to keep our promises. Please help us to be people who can always be trusted to do the things that we say we will do. Amen

17

Mending friendships: forgiveness

Aim: To consider the importance of making friends again after falling out.

You will need: A box containing a variety of objects or pictures of objects that need mending, along with items that could be used to mend them. For example:

- a broken pen/glue
- a shirt with a missing button/needle and thread
- a picture of a cut finger/a plaster
- a torn certificate/sticky tape.

You may like to use pictures of more complicated examples, such as a broken wire and soldering iron, a punctured bicycle tyre and repair kit, or a crack in a wall and bucket of cement.

Assembly outline

Ask volunteers to come forward to hold the broken objects. Invite the children to look closely at the objects and spot the connection. When they have realised that each one is broken in some way, ask how each of them could be mended. When a child names the way in which a broken object could be mended, ask them to select the correct item from the box and stand next to the appropriate broken object.

Ask the children if they can think of any other examples of things that have been broken and mended again. It may be that some children have had broken bones. Point out that sometimes it doesn't bother us when things get broken, but sometimes it makes us feel sad. For example, if a button falls off a shirt or we get a hole in our tights, we may not feel too bothered. However, if we break our favourite toy or even break a bone, we can feel hurt and upset.

Explain that sometimes people speak about things being broken that we can't physically see. People who are very sad could be described as 'broken-hearted'. This doesn't mean that their heart has really broken; it means that they are very, very sad. Often it is love and care that can help people recover from a broken heart.

We can also describe friendships as being broken. Ask the children what they think a 'broken friendship' means. Explain that sometimes we have disagreements and mis-understandings with our friends that cause us to become upset and not to want to spend time with that person any more. Unfortunately, friendships can't be mended with glue or a needle and thread. Ask the children to think about how broken friendships might be mended.

Explain that, often, friendships can be mended by saying 'sorry' and being willing to forgive. Say that no one finds it easy to admit that they are wrong and say 'sorry'. However, when we do, we usually find that people respect us more and are willing to have us back as a friend. Ask the children to pause for a moment and think about whether they need to say 'sorry' to anyone. Encourage them to do this later, if necessary.

Ask the children if they think it is easy to forgive another person. Explain that when someone hurts us, it can be very difficult to forgive them. Sometimes we are so upset that we feel as if we can hurt them back by not being friends with them again. However, if we refuse to forgive, we usually end up hurting ourselves more.

Ask the children to think for a moment about whether there is someone they need to forgive. Challenge them to forgive that person today. Explain that sometimes, when people have hurt us, it can take a while to build the friendship up again, but with time and effort it is possible to mend the friendship.

What the Bible says

The Bible records an occasion when Peter, one of the disciples, came to Jesus and asked how many times he should forgive someone who had done something wrong to him. Peter asked Jesus if he should forgive the person up to seven times. Jesus replied that he should still forgive even if the person had wronged him 77 times (**Matthew 18:21–22**).

The Bible speaks a lot about forgiveness and encourages us to forgive other people in the same way that God is willing to forgive us. **Ephesians 4:32** says, 'Be kind and compassionate to one another, forgiving each other, just as in Christ God forgave you.'

Pause for thought

Pause for a moment and think about your friends. What is it that makes them special? Think about what you could do to show them that you care. Have you fallen out with a friend recently? Have you done something to hurt or upset them? Why not go and mend the friendship? It may mean that you have to say 'sorry' or forgive them for upsetting you, but friendships are too precious to allow them to remain broken.

PRAYER

Dear God, thank you for all our friends. Thank you for times when we can laugh and have fun together. Thank you for times when we can be quiet together and care for one another. Please help us to be good friends. Help us to be quick to sort out problems and always be willing to forgive. Amen

18

Peace

Aim: To consider the meaning of the word 'peace'.

You will need: The word 'peace' on a screen or written on paper in large letters; a dictionary; a drum; a sun lounger or chair; gentle recorded music (if possible, the sound of waves or rippling water); a packet of jelly babies.

Assembly outline

Invite a volunteer to hold up the word 'peace'. Ask the children what they think the word means. Invite another volunteer to look up the word 'peace' in the dictionary and read out the meanings. Explain that the word 'peace' can be used in many situations, and during this assembly you want to think about five of the different meanings.

Ask for a volunteer to come to the front, and give them a drum. Explain that when you lift your hand in the air, you want them to play the drum loudly; and when you lower your hand, you want them to stop. Lift your hand and encourage the child to play loudly for a few seconds before stopping them. Explain that the first meaning of 'peace' is the absence of noise. If a class is being noisy, a teacher may say, 'Please can we have a bit of peace.' A parent may put the children to bed and say, 'Now I can have a bit of peace!'

With the drummer child remaining at the front, ask for another volunteer. Ask this child to lie on the sun lounger or sit on the chair in a relaxed manner. Switch on the gentle music and invite all the children to listen to it for a minute with their eyes closed. Ask the children how they are feeling and how they think the person on the lounger feels. Can they imagine whereabouts the person on the sun lounger could be? (Examples could be at the beach, in the garden or beside a swimming pool.) Explain that, as well as the absence of noise, the word 'peace' means calmness and restfulness. If we are in a still, quiet and relaxing setting, we will often describe it as peaceful.

With the first two children remaining at the front, call for two further volunteers and ask them to stand facing each other in a way that suggests they have had a serious argument. Explain that when friends have arguments and fall out with each other, sometimes another person needs to step in and help them 'make peace' with each other. Ask the children what they think the term 'make peace' means. Explain that making peace means sorting out a dispute or problem between people so that they can become friends again.

Ask if they have heard the term 'peacemakers'. What do they think it means? Explain that we all have a role to play as 'peacemakers'. If we are peacemakers, we won't wind other people up and try to get them frustrated or cross. We won't try to annoy each other, and we won't try to pick faults in each other and get people into trouble. Instead we will try to help others, look for the good in others and help people stay friends with each other.

Explain that for the fourth meaning of 'peace' you need someone to come to the front to hold the bag of jelly babies. Explain that jelly babies were first produced in 1918, just after the end of World War I. At this time, they were called 'peace babies'. Explain that the fourth meaning of the word 'peace' is a time when there is no war.

Quickly recap each meaning of the word 'peace', then say that the final meaning you are going to think about is 'inner peace'. Ask the children what they think this term means. Explain that inner peace means feeling peaceful and content on the inside. Everyone has times when they feel worried, stressed, agitated and upset, but we shouldn't feel that way all the time. If we do constantly feel like this, it is a good idea to talk to a teacher and explain how we feel. Sometimes talking about things can make us feel much better.

Ask the children to think about their lives and the life of the school. Encourage them to think about what they can do to help the world be a more peaceful place.

What the Bible says

In **Matthew 8:23–27** and **Mark 4:35–41** we read about Jesus calming a storm. While the disciples were sailing across the Sea of Galilee, Jesus fell asleep in the back of the boat. Suddenly a great storm arose and the disciples were terrified that they were going to drown. Eventually one of them woke Jesus. Jesus stood and said to the waves, 'Be still.' Immediately the storm stopped and everything was calm and peaceful.

The Bible also encourages us to be peacemakers. **Romans 12:18** tells us, 'If it is possible, as far as it depends on you, live at peace with everyone.'

Pause for thought

Do you feel peaceful in your own life? Are you worried or anxious about anything? If you are, why not decide to talk to a teacher today? Are you living at peace with other people or do you need to 'make peace' with anyone? If you do, then try to sort it out and make friends quickly.

PRAYER

Dear God, sometimes we feel sad and worried. When we feel this way, please help us to have the courage to talk to someone about it. Please also help us to make every effort to live at peace with other people. Please be close to people today who live in areas where wars are being fought. Bring them peace. Amen

Perseverance

Aim: To consider the need to keep on persevering even when we feel like giving up.

You will need: Pictures of three or four very familiar objects (for example, a lion, a chair, a banana and a tree); a picture of a less familiar object (such as a snail); a prearranged adult volunteer; hula hoops; skipping ropes.

The first three or four objects should be easy to guess by asking questions. The fifth picture should be slightly more difficult to guess.

Your adult volunteer needs to act as if they are trying to guess the picture on the fifth card, although in reality they will be getting it wrong on purpose. The idea is that they keep on persevering.

Assembly outline

Ask the children if they can think of a time when they found a skill very difficult to achieve. Maybe they couldn't skip, hop, hula-hoop, complete a maths question, make friends or learn to read.

Ask if anyone remembers a time when they couldn't hop, although now they have learnt how to do it. Invite a few of these children to come to the front to demonstrate. Ask them how they moved from being unable to hop to being able to do it.

Ask if anyone used to find it difficult to skip, although now they can do it. Call a few of these children to demonstrate. Then repeat the process for hula-hooping. You may like to challenge the volunteers to see who can skip and hula-hoop for the longest time. Explain that these children had a choice when they realised there was something they couldn't do: they could either give up or they could keep on trying.

Explain that you are going to play a game. You will ask a volunteer to come to the front, and you will then show the rest of the children a picture (for example, of an animal, a household object, a vehicle, a type of food and so on). The volunteer will try to find out what the picture shows, by asking questions that can be answered only with 'yes' or 'no'. For example, if the picture is of a bed, the questions could be:

- Is it an animal? (No)
- Is it a vehicle? (No)
- Is it something in a house? (Yes)
- Is it a piece of furniture? (Yes)
- Would you find it in the kitchen? (No)
- Would you find it in the bathroom? (No)
- Would you find it in a bedroom? (Yes)
- Is it a wardrobe? (No)
- Is it a bed? (Yes)

Ask for a volunteer and show the remaining children the first picture. Invite the volunteer to begin to ask questions. If they are struggling to think of a question, either whisper a suggestion to them or ask the other children to suggest a question to ask (without giving the answer away). For example, they might suggest questions about whether the picture shows an animal, is a kind of food, is big or small or makes a noise.

After the first volunteer has guessed correctly, invite the prearranged adult to come forward. Show the children the fifth, more difficult, picture and ask the adult to begin to guess. Make sure the adult is prepared to ask questions that will *not* lead to the correct answer. After a while, suggest that, as the adult is taking so long, you are going to let another child have a go at guessing a different picture and you will come back to the adult later. Don't let the adult sit down, or a child will probably whisper the answer to them!

When the second child volunteer has guessed correctly, invite the adult to have another go. This process should be repeated until three or four children have correctly guessed their pictures, with the adult having another try between each child. Eventually tell the adult that they can have two more guesses—and on the second guess they should correctly identify the picture. The adult should cheer, look delighted or even complete a lap of honour round the room.

Ask the children which of the volunteers they thought found it the easiest to guess the picture. Ask them which of the volunteers found it the most difficult: the answer will be the adult.

Ask the adult how they felt when they kept getting the answer wrong. They should explain that they felt bad and felt like giving up. However, they decided to keep on trying. Ask how they feel now that they have guessed correctly.

Explain that we would say that the adult 'persevered'. Perseverance means that we keep on trying, even when we feel like giving up. Refer back to the children who showed their hopping, skipping and hula-hooping skills earlier. Point out that, at some stage, each of them probably felt like giving up, but they carried on trying: they persevered.

Explain that each of us is tempted to give up in difficult situations. When we feel like this, we have a choice to make—to give up or to persevere. Remind the children that when we persevere, we keep hoping that the next time we try the skill, that will be the time when we actually succeed.

What the Bible says

The Bible tells us that when we feel like giving up, we can ask God for help. Christians believe that God is always there for them and will give them strength in times of need. **Philippians 4:13** says, 'I can do all this through him who gives me strength.'

The Bible also tells us that although some things are impossible for us to do, nothing is impossible for God. **Matthew 19:26** says, 'Jesus looked at them and said, "With man this is impossible, but with God all things are possible."' God can help us with the most difficult of problems.

Pause for thought

Is there something that you are finding difficult at the moment? Do you feel like giving up? Remember that you never know if the next time you attempt it will be the time you manage to do it. Don't give up! Make the decision to keep on persevering and never stop trying.

PRAYER

Dear God, sometimes we come across things that we find difficult. Sometimes we feel like giving up. Please help us always to keep on trying, and help us to encourage other people to do the same. Amen

20

Responsibility

Aim: To consider that each of us is responsible for the world around us.

You will need: Pieces of paper with different responsibilities written on them in large letters; a card with the word 'Responsibility' written on it in large letters; a dictionary; a globe or map of the world.

Examples of different responsibilities might be:

- making the playground a pleasant place to be
- helping people in poorer countries to have clean water to drink
- making new children or visitors feel welcome in school
- protecting endangered species of animals
- helping to reduce global warming

Change the responsibilities shown to fit in with the school and age range.

Assembly outline

Invite a volunteer to hold up the word 'Responsibility' and ask the children what they think it means. When they have given their ideas, ask a child to look up the definition of 'responsibility' in the dictionary and read it out loud. You may want to write the definition on a board for everyone to read together.

Ask the children if they have any responsibilities in school, at home or in any other place. Examples could include membership of the school council or a scout company, being the register monitor or book monitor and making their bed each day.

Explain that you have a number of responsibilities written on pieces of paper. Ask a volunteer to hold up the first piece of paper and invite someone to read it out loud. Ask the children if they think they have any part in fulfilling the responsibility shown. For example, do they have any responsibility for 'making the playground a pleasant place to be'? Discuss each responsibility in turn, asking the children for their ideas.

It will seem obvious to the children that certain things are their responsibility—for example, keeping the school grounds tidy, making the playground a pleasant place or making their beds. However, the aim of the assembly is to help them see that each of us has a responsibility for the wider world in which we live. We can help to reduce global warming by switching off lights and not wasting electricity; we can help to provide clean water for people in other countries by helping with charity events, and so on.

Show the children the globe or map of the world. Point out where we live and say how small our country seems, compared to the rest of the world. Say that even though we seem small, our actions can have far-reaching effects. For example, by doing things that add to global warming, we are helping to melt the ice caps, which in turn destroys habitats and prevents animals from living there.

Explain that sometimes we know we have a responsibility, but we forget or choose not to take that responsibility seriously. We may know that we should hold the door open for a visitor but we are in such a rush to play with our friends that we run outside without thinking about the people behind us. We may desperately want to buy some sweets and football cards, so we block out the thought that the school is having a charity collection to provide clean water for people in poorer countries. We may know that we have left the lights on in the classroom or our bedroom, but we decide it is too much effort to go back and switch them off. In these ways, we choose not to take our responsibilities seriously.

Add that as we get older we will have more responsibilities, but all of us are responsible in some way, no matter what age we are. Each of us can do our bit to make the world a better place for everyone to live in.

Challenge the children to realise that each of us is responsible for the world in which we live. Each of us is responsible in some way for the people we see every day, and each of us can make a difference, however small, to the rest of the world.

What the Bible says

The book of Psalms includes many poems that speak about the beauty of the world. **Psalm 24:1** says, 'The earth is the Lord's, and everything in it, the world, and all who live in it.' Christians believe that God created the world and every person in it. They believe that we all have a part to play in caring for the world. The Bible also encourages us to be unselfish in our actions and to think about the value of other people. **Philippians 2:3** says, 'Value others above yourselves.' If we see the value of other people and the value of the world, then we will take our responsibilities towards them seriously.

Pause for thought

Think for a moment about any responsibility you have. Are you a monitor for something or a member of the school council? Are you responsible for keeping the school grounds tidy? Are you responsible for making school a pleasant place to be? All of us are responsible for something. Make a decision today to play your part in making the world a better place for all of us to live in.

PRAYER

Dear God, thank you for the beauty of the world. Please help us to do all that we can to protect it and keep it beautiful. Thank you for our homes, schools, families and friends. Help us to play our part in caring for them and making the world a happier place. Amen

21

Rules

Aim: To consider that rules are important if people are to be safe and enjoy life to the full.

This assembly works well at the start of a new school year.

You will need: Large pieces of paper with different rules written on them, *or* downloaded pictures of familiar road signs; coloured cards with 'What?', 'Why?' and 'What if?' written on them; a dictionary; a list of class or school rules.

Choose rules with which the children will be familiar—for example, no running in the corridor; do not park in front of the gate; do not shout out in lessons; please close the door; no smoking.

Assembly outline

Ask the children what they think the word 'rule' means. Once they have expressed their ideas, invite a child to look up the definition in the dictionary. (There will be a number of different definitions available: you are looking for the one implying a set of regulations about a specific activity.)

Ask the children if they can think of any rules that they have seen around school or elsewhere. Explain that you are going to show them some different rules and you want them to think about three questions: 'What?', 'Why?' and 'What if?' Call three children to the front to hold up the coloured cards.

Invite a volunteer to hold up the first rule and ask someone to read it out loud. Point to the 'What?' card and ask what the rule means. Point to the 'Why?' card and ask why someone would have thought of this rule. Point to the 'What if?' card and ask what could happen if the rule was not put in place or not followed.

For example, if the rule is 'Do not park in front of the gate', the 'What?' question is straightforward: the rule means simply that the owner of the gate does not want anyone to park in front of it. The answer to the 'Why?' question could be that the owner needs to drive out of the gate and is unable to do so if a car is parked there. The 'What if?' question might lead to the answer that the owner might be unable to drive out of the gate in an emergency if it is blocked by a parked car.

If the rule is 'No running in the corridors', again the 'What?' question is straightforward: no one should run in the corridor. 'Why?' Because it is dangerous. 'What if?' People may collide with each other or get knocked over if the rule is ignored.

Ask different children to hold up the remaining questions and talk through the 'What? Why? What if?' questions for each rule.

Say that sometimes we can feel as if rules are bad things because they stop us from taking actions that we consider to be fun. For example, it may be fun to run down the corridor—but it is safer to obey the rule. It may be fun to shout out answers in class—but, if we obey the rule, lessons run more smoothly, everyone gets a chance to answer, the teacher does not get cross and everyone is happier.

Remind the children that rules are put in place with the aim of making things better for everybody. They are not there to stop us having fun; they aim to make things the best for everybody.

Point out that rules are most likely to be kept if the people they affect have some part in deciding what the rules will be. If it is the start of a new school year, you may like to discuss what rules would be good in school generally, or in the classroom. If the assembly doesn't coincide with the start of a new term or year, you could encourage the children to think of rules for games in the playground.

You may like to ask the children to design some posters which can be displayed around school reminding people of various school rules.

What the Bible says

In the Old Testament part of the Bible (written before the birth of Jesus), there is a special set of rules called the ten commandments. Christians believe that these rules were given to Moses by God. The story is found in **Exodus 20:1–17**. These rules guide us both in our attitudes towards God and in the way we should treat other people.

In the New Testament part of the Bible (written after the birth of Jesus), in **Matthew 22:37–40**, Jesus speaks about the two greatest commandments or rules, which are 'Love the Lord your God with all your heart and with all your soul and with all your mind' and 'Love your neighbour as yourself.' Jesus explains that all the rules that God has given can be summed up in these two commandments.

Pause for thought

Sometimes rules can seem as if they are there to stop us having fun, but really they are there to keep us safe and to help us enjoy life more. Think for a moment about some of the rules that we have for our school or classroom. (Read a few of them out.) Some of the rules are to keep us safe; some are to help us all get on with our work better; some are to help us all stay friends together. Are there any rules that you struggle to keep? Pause for a moment to think about the importance of those rules. Why not make a special effort this week to keep the rules and make the school an even better place?

PRAYER

Dear God, please help us to see that rules are important. Help us to realise that they are there to help us and to make our lives more enjoyable. Please help us to think about other people and always behave in a way that will help them. Amen

22

Seasons

Aim: To consider how each season is special and full of exciting things to experience and enjoy.

You will need: Four large pieces of paper with the words 'Autumn', 'Winter', 'Spring' and 'Summer' written on them; lots of small pictures on card, related to the four seasons (see suggestions below); sticky tack or double-sided tape.

Season-related pictures could include:

- Autumn: different coloured leaves, bonfire, fireworks, conkers, gloves, harvest
- Winter: snow, Christmas tree, snowman, Christmas decorations, tinsel, tree with no leaves
- Spring: flowers, blossom trees, lambs, chicks, Easter eggs
- Summer: bucket and spade, sun, sunglasses, swimming costume, ice cream, beach.

There should be equal numbers of pictures for each season.

Assembly outline

Before the assembly begins, position the pictures around the room. They may be placed face-up or face-down depending on the age of the children and the time available.

Divide the children into four teams. Ask them if they can name the seasons of the year. Allocate the name of one season to each of the teams and invite a member of each team to come forward to hold up the corresponding large piece of paper, as a team banner. Call for three more team members to come to the front and sit beside their team banner.

Ask the children what sorts of things they associate with each season. Explain that before the assembly began, you placed lots of small cards around the room, showing pictures of things that you would expect to see in the different seasons. There are equal numbers of cards for each season: tell the children how many there are of each.

When you indicate, one of the three seated volunteers in each team should stand up and look for a picture that matches their team's season. When they find a suitable picture, they should stick it on to their banner and sit down. The next child in the team will then get up and look for another picture. This process should be repeated until one of the teams has found all their cards.

Make it clear that if the children see a card belonging to a different team, they must leave it where it is. The winning team is the first to have all the season cards attached to their banner. You may like to play music while the children look for the cards.

Once all the cards have been collected, ask the children to think about which of the seasons they like best. Ask who likes the summer best and choose one child to explain why this is their choice. Repeat for every season.

Point out that every season has something special about it. If all the seasons were identical, we would miss out on the excitement and variety that we enjoy.

Say that when we speak about seasons, we are usually referring to the different times of the year. However, we can also refer to different seasons of our lives. We could describe our childhood as one season, and our teenage years as another. We may speak about the season of life when we are having our own families, or when our children have left home, or when we retire. All of these times in our lives can be both exciting and slightly daunting. However, just as the seasons of the year continue to happen and we can't do anything to stop them changing, so too we can't do anything about the seasons of our lives. We will all grow into teenagers and then adults. We will leave primary school, then leave secondary school, and then go to university or get a job.

Remind the children that the most important thing is to remember that every season of our lives can be wonderfully exciting, with new adventures and experiences waiting for us wherever we go.

What the Bible says

Seasons are mentioned in the first book of the Bible. In **Genesis 8:22** we read that 'seedtime and harvest, cold and heat, summer and winter, day and night will never cease'.

The Bible also speaks about the seasons of our lives. **Ecclesiastes 3:1** says, 'There is a time for everything, and a season for every activity under the heavens.' However, the writer goes on to reassure us that, even though everything may change, God will always be there.

Pause for thought

What do you like best about springtime? Is it the lambs prancing around in the fields or the excitement of seeing Easter eggs appearing in the shops? What is your favourite part of summer? Maybe the long days and the chance to play at the beach. What do you like about autumn and winter? Maybe the nights drawing in and the beautiful colours on the trees, or the excitement of Christmas as the lights and trees appear in the shop windows. Never forget that the seasons of life are even more exciting than the seasons of the year. They are full of surprises that can bring joy and new experiences.

PRAYER

Dear God, thank you for the seasons of the year and for the special things that happen in each of them. Please help us to be full of excitement as we move through every season of our lives. Thank you that you never change and that you are always there beside us. Amen

23

Seeing the good

Aim: To encourage the children to look for the hidden beauty that can be found in both people and situations.

You will need: A bin liner full of clean rubbish (such as plastic bottles, cardboard boxes and so on); a pile of books; a table; a pile of PE kits or bags; two small gifts (such as bars of chocolate) wrapped in gold, silver or bright paper; an envelope containing a card written to the children, stating how lovely they are and how proud you are of them.

Assembly outline

Before the children arrive, tip the bin liner on its side so that the rubbish is partially falling out. Position the books so that they look as if they have fallen off the table. Position the PE bags on the floor so that it looks as if they have been left in a big mess. Hide the small gifts among the books and PE kits, and hide the card amid the rubbish. Although the gifts and card should be mainly hidden, it is important that a small corner of each can be seen when the children look more closely.

As the children arrive in the hall, make sure that they see you looking at the mess with a concerned expression on your face. Once they have settled down, ask them if they noticed anything unusual as they arrived. When they point out that there are a lot of things on the floor, draw their attention first to the untidy pile of books. Ask what they think could have happened here to cause such a mess. Move on to the pile of PE kits. Ask the children if any of them have made this mess and what they think could have happened. Move to stand beside the bag of rubbish and ask if the children think the room looks better with all the mess spread out over it.

Invite the children to put up their hands if they like having 'rubbish' spread everywhere. Ask if they would like the mess to remain where it is or if they would like it to be cleared up. Say that most people don't like rubbish spread everywhere; most people don't want their school to be an untidy, unclean place.

All the children will have assumed that there was simply a mess at the front of the room, and no one will have looked more closely. Ask for a volunteer to come and examine the pile of books. When they notice the wrapped present, ask them to pull it out, and tell them that they can keep it. Point out that the books looked like a mess that had been knocked on to the floor, but inside was a present that was worth having.

Ask for a volunteer to look more closely at the pile of PE kits. When they discover the present, ask them to pull it out and keep it. Say that if the volunteer hadn't looked more closely, they would never have discovered the present.

Now ask for a volunteer to look more closely at the rubbish. The child will probably be looking for bright, shiny paper, like the first two presents. When they can't see any shiny paper, ask them to look more closely and, if necessary, guide them towards the envelope. Ask the child to open the envelope and read the note inside.

Explain that, in all three situations, people assumed they were looking at something unattractive and messy. However, hidden in each pile was something worth looking for. The first two contained presents and the last one contained a note that made the children feel special.

Point out that all of us can be quick to talk about the faults that we see in other people. We find it easy to notice the things that people do badly or wrong. However, we often find it difficult to stop and look more closely at people so that we can see the good things about them. Explain that even though our friends do things wrong, we can be quick to overlook their faults because we naturally get on with them and like them. However, with people that we find more difficult to like, we tend to be more impatient and are sometimes so quick to judge them that everything they do can seem annoying or wrong.

Ask the children to think about someone in school whom they don't know very well or have found difficult to get along with in the past. Make the suggestion that if they went and talked to that person or asked them to join in a game, they might be surprised at how much they like them.

What the Bible says

Although the Bible encourages us to stand up against what is wrong, it also encourages us always to look for good in other people. There are some famous words in **Philippians 4:8**, which say, 'Whatever is true, whatever is noble, whatever is right, whatever is pure, whatever is lovely, whatever is admirable—if anything is excellent or praiseworthy—think about such things.' Sometimes it is easy to focus on other people's faults rather than noticing the good things about them. If we make an effort to think about people's good points, rather than the things we don't like, it will make a difference to our relationships with them.

Pause for thought

Do you find it much easier to look for bad things in people and to point out their faults? Pause for a moment to think about these words from Philippians. Whatever your beliefs about God, these words are powerful. If everyone in school tried to look for something lovely, good or praiseworthy in everybody else, school would be an even happier place to be.

PRAYER

Dear God, thank you for the people we meet each day. Sometimes it is easier to look at people's faults and complain about the things that we don't like. Please help us to try to see good things in other people, in the same way that we hope others will see the good things in us. Amen

24

Sharing

Aim: To consider the importance of sharing with other people.

You will need: A bag containing a banana, a wrapped cereal bar and a carton of juice with a straw; a pair of scissors.

Assembly outline

Tell the children that you have been so busy this morning, you haven't had time to eat your breakfast. (Change the time of day and meal according to the timing of the assembly.) Explain that you are extremely hungry so you are going to have to eat your breakfast now. Apologise for eating in front of the children, but point out that it is very important to have a good breakfast.

Pull a banana out of your bag. Peel the banana and begin to eat it. After a few bites, look round guiltily and say that you feel rather selfish eating in front of all the children and you wonder if anyone would like half of your banana. Invite a child to the front, finish peeling the banana and give the skin to the child. While they are looking disappointed or confused, tell the rest of the children how generous you have been in sharing the banana.

Next, take the wrapped cereal bar from your bag. Explain that you are still hungry so you are going to eat a cereal bar. Ask if anyone would like to share it with you, and choose a child to come to the front. Unwrap the bar and comment on how shiny and brightly coloured the wrapper is. Give the wrapper to the child and, while they look disappointed, emphasise to the other children that you are being very kind, sharing with others.

Finally, take the carton of juice from your bag. Hold it up and say that you would like to share it with someone. Ask if anyone is thirsty and invite a child to the front. Take the straw off the carton and hand it to the child, assuring them that they can keep it. Use the scissors to cut the corner off the carton and then drink the contents.

Ask the seated children why they think the three children at the front don't look very happy. When someone says that you were meant to be sharing your food and drink with them, refer to each child in turn, pointing out that you did what you said you would. You shared part of the banana with the first child, you shared part of the wrapped cereal bar with the second and you shared part of the carton with the third.

Admit that although, in one sense, you did share what you had with the three children, what you actually did was selfish and not very kind. Explain that real sharing means considering other people and their needs rather than what we want for ourselves. Sometimes it is difficult to be a good sharer. Sometimes it is easy to do a tiny amount of sharing but to keep hold of the best things for ourselves. We might give a friend a ball to play with at break time, knowing that we have already hidden the best ball for ourselves. We might say that a child can play with us, but we give them a part to play in the game that no one else wants. We might share out some food and give someone we don't like a much smaller amount than one of our friends gets.

Say that real sharing begins with the attitude that everyone we meet is worth sharing with. Point out that when we share with others, it can make us feel happy because we can see the joy that we have brought to someone else.

What the Bible says

The Bible teaches us that God wants us to think of other people as being very important. **Hebrews 13:16** says, 'Do not forget to do good and to share with others.' Sometimes it is easy to forget to do good things. In this verse, the Bible encourages us to remember to do good and to share, rather than being too busy looking after ourselves and trying to get what we want.

Pause for thought

How easy do you find it to share? Can you think of a time when you didn't want to share what you had with others? Can you think of a time today when you might have the opportunity to share? Could you share the equipment at break time, share your friends with other people, share a job that you enjoy doing or share a game that you are playing? Can you think of one thing that you could share today?

PRAYER

Dear God, thank you for everything that we have and for all the people who share with us. Sometimes it is hard to share with those around us. Please help us to learn to be generous. Help us to realise that all of us can make the world a happier place by sharing what we have. Amen

25

Standing up for yourself

Aim: To encourage the children to think before they follow the behaviour of others and to have the courage to stand up for themselves.

You will need to know: the rules of the two games below.

Simon says

The teacher gives simple instructions and the children only follow the instructions if the words 'Simon says...' are spoken first. For example:

- Teacher: 'Simon says, "Put both hands in the air"': the children carry out the instruction.
- Teacher: 'Simon says, "Stand on one leg"': the children carry out the instruction.
- Teacher: 'Sit down': the children do not carry out the instruction but remain standing on one leg.

This and that

The teacher shows actions for the children to follow, while saying either 'Do this' or 'Do that'. If the teacher says, 'Do this', the children copy the action; if the teacher says, 'Do that', the children do not copy it. For example:

- Teacher: 'Do this…' (and places hands on head): the children copy the action.
- Teacher: 'Do this…' (and claps hands): the children copy the action.
- Teacher: 'Do that…' (stops clapping and places hands on knees): the children do not copy the action but continue to clap.

These games can continue in two ways: either all the children continue to join in even if they incorrectly follow an instruction or copy an action, or those who respond incorrectly are out and the teacher continues with the instructions or actions until a winner is found.

Assembly outline

Explain that you are going to have some fun in the assembly today and you will begin by playing two games. Explain the rules for 'Simon says…' so that you are sure all of the children know how to play. Play the game as described above. It can be played just for fun or to produce a winner.

Explain the rules for 'This and that' so that you are sure all of the children know how to play. Play the game as described above. Again, it can be played for fun or to produce a winner.

Say that in both these games the children were following you as a leader. Sometimes they were following words and sometimes they were following actions. The children trusted that you would not ask them to do anything that would be inappropriate, dangerous or wrong. They knew that they could follow you safely. Explain that every day, often without thinking, we follow other people's words and actions. Sometimes this is a good thing, but sometimes it is not so good. If we see someone being kind, caring, hardworking and polite, it is good to follow them, but if we see others being unkind, rude and unfriendly, it is unwise to follow them.

Ask the children if they have ever been in a situation where they had to decide whether to follow good or bad behaviour. You are not going to ask them what those situations were, but you want them to think about how they reacted when faced with a decision. Give a few appropriate examples:

- A child was messing around in the classroom and not getting on with their work. Did the other children join in or ignore the bad behaviour?
- A child was being nasty to someone in the playground. Did the other children stop them and try to be kind to the child who was being picked on?

Ask the children why they think people often follow the leader in situations like these. Say that sometimes we follow bad examples because we want to be popular, we want to make people laugh, we don't want to be picked on ourselves or we want to feel important. Sometimes it can be very hard to stand up for ourselves and for what we feel is right. To stand up for what is right takes courage. It might mean that we are not so popular and that people make fun of us, but we will feel good on the inside, and in the long run others will respect us far more.

What the Bible says

There were many times when Jesus stood up for people, even when it made him unpopular. **Luke 19:1–10** tells how Jesus spent time with a tax collector called Zacchaeus. Zacchaeus used to steal money from people and was very unpopular. Despite this, Jesus took the trouble to get to know him and, as a result, Zacchaeus' life was changed. There are also many times recorded in the Bible when Jesus spoke out against things that he believed to be wrong.

Pause for thought

Would you rather follow other people's bad examples so that you can be popular, or stand up for what is good and right? Are there times when you have joined in bad behaviour or done something that you felt bad about, because you wanted to fit in with the crowd? Why not make a decision today to follow good examples and to stand up for what is good?

PRAYER

Dear God, please help us to follow good examples. Help us to think about what we say and how we act, and help us to have the courage to make our own choices and not simply to follow the crowd. Amen

26

Think before you speak

Aim: To consider the importance of thinking carefully about the things that we say.

You will need: The words 'Yes' and 'No' written on two separate cards; volunteers to play the 'Yes, No' game.

Be ready to ask quick-fire questions to the volunteers, with the aim of getting them to say the word 'Yes' or 'No'.

Assembly outline

Show the children the two cards and ask someone to read the words out loud. Invite a volunteer to come forward to play a game. Explain that you are going to ask lots of questions to which they can give any answer they want, but they must *not* say the word 'Yes' or 'No'. (Make it clear that saying words like 'Yep', 'Nope' or 'Yeah', or shaking/ nodding their head, counts as saying 'Yes' or 'No'.)

Your aim is to trick the volunteer into saying 'Yes' or 'No' as quickly as possible. The best way to do this is to be quite casual and try to stop them concentrating. The volunteer must give their answers quickly.

For example:

- Teacher: So what is your name?
- Volunteer: James.
- Teacher: James, that's a nice name. So how old are you, James?
- Volunteer: Nine.
- Teacher: So that means you're in Mr Smith's class?
- Volunteer: I am.
- Teacher: Do you like it in that class?
- Volunteer: I do.
- Teacher: What's your favourite subject?
- Volunteer: Maths.
- Teacher: Maths?
- Volunteer: Yes.

The volunteer is out.

Invite a number of different children to have a go. You may like to invite a couple of older children to work together to catch you out.

Explain that, in the game, the person asking the questions is trying to make the volunteer speak before they have thought properly about their answer. Speaking before we have thought about what we are going to say is a common problem.

Ask the children if they can remember a time when they wished they had kept quiet rather than saying something out loud. Examples may be answering back to a parent or teacher, which led to them getting into trouble; being cross with a friend and saying something unkind that the friend still remembers; breaking a promise and so on. Explain that it is very easy to speak before we think, but it often gets us into trouble in some way. It would be far better to pause and think about the effect that our words might have.

Point out that, as well as making sure our words don't get us into trouble, we can use words positively, in ways that are helpful to other people. We can choose how we use our words. In a PE lesson, we can choose to shout at others if they don't perform as well as we do, or we can choose to be encouraging. If a particular child is placed on our team, we can choose whether to complain or whether to welcome them. We can choose to say kind things or to be unkind. We can choose to talk about others behind their backs and spread gossip or rumours about them, or we can choose to say only good things about other people. We have a choice.

Encourage the children to pause before they speak, and decide whether the words they are about to say will help both themselves and others.

What the Bible says

The Bible has a lot to say about the way we use our mouths. Probably the best-known passage about how we use words is found in the letter of James. (It is thought that this letter was written by James, the brother of Jesus.) In **James 3:1–12** he writes about the power of the tongue, comparing it to a spark that sets off a huge fire, or a small rudder that moves a huge ship. What this means is that even the small words that come out of our mouths can have a massive effect on other people.

Pause for thought

Ask the children to close their eyes and think for a moment about a time when words have either hurt them or have led to others being hurt. For example, they may have said something that directly upset someone else or they could have spoken too quickly and got in trouble as a result. Ask them to consider what would have happened if they had stopped and thought about the consequences of their words.

Challenge the children to pause before they speak this week. Remind them that the way we use words is a choice for us to make. Challenge them to make the decision that each day they will say one thing to another person that will make that person feel good.

PRAYER

Dear God, please help us to use our mouths for the good of other people. Please help us to think before we speak, so that we say things that encourage others, rather than making them feel upset or hurt in any way. Amen

27

Values

Aim: To consider which things are of real value in the world.

You will need: A medal podium constructed in any safe way; a cover for the podium; a variety of objects or pictures showing things or people that may be considered to range in importance (for example, money, jewellery, a teddy bear, a jar of jam, a picture of a doctor, a photo of a baby, a packet of biscuits, some water, a coat, a picture of a famous celebrity).

To make your podium, stage blocks work well, but you could use a large cardboard cut-out or even chairs and tables of different levels. The podium will have articles placed on it but the children will not stand on it. If possible, the podium should be covered before the assembly begins.

Your choice of objects or pictures does not matter, as long as there is a good range that will allow the children to evaluate importance.

Assembly outline

Show the children the covered podium and ask them to guess what is underneath. You could give them clues, such as, 'The object underneath this cover has three different levels; you may see something like this at the Olympic Games; usually three people stand on this object' and so on. Invite a volunteer to remove the cover. Ask the children where they have seen a podium before and what it is used for.

Explain that a podium is used at sporting events for presenting medals to the people who came in first, second and third places. The person in first place will stand on the highest level. Say that you are going to use the podium to help the children think about the importance of different things in their lives. Explain that you are going to show them some different objects or pictures and you want them to think about how important each one is and then vote to decide where it will be placed on the podium. The most important objects will be placed at the top level, the least important on the bottom level and everything else in between.

Show the children one of the objects. Ask them what it is, what it is used for and how important it is. Lead the discussion before asking the children to vote, by a show of hands, on where on the podium the object should be placed. Ask a child to position the object at the level agreed by the vote.

For example, show the children the teddy bear and ask them if it is important. Some children may think that the teddy is very important, as they don't like to go to sleep without their bear. Some may think it is unimportant because they don't like cuddly toys. You could point out that the teddy was given to you by your grandparents when you were born, and that may change the children's opinions.

Repeat the process with each article. The levels at which the objects are placed are not too important, as the main aim is to help the children think about the importance of things in their lives.

Once all the objects are positioned, ask the children if they can think of anything in their own lives that should be placed on the top of the podium. You are really asking them what things are the most important in their lives. It is likely that the discussions will lead to the idea that material possessions are not as important as people.

Challenge the children about how they treat people and material possessions. Ask how they can show people that they are valued.

What the Bible says

The Bible speaks a lot about the value of people. There are many passages telling us about God's love for people. **John 3:16** says, 'For God so loved the world that he gave his one and only Son,' and **John 15:13** says, 'Greater love has no one than this: to lay down one's life for one's friends.' The Bible is not against people being rich or having lots of material possessions, but it does warn against allowing those possessions to become too important. A well-known passage, **Matthew 6:19–20**, says, 'Do not store up for yourselves treasures on earth, where moths and vermin destroy, and where thieves break in and steal. But store up for yourselves treasures in heaven.'

Pause for thought

What is the most important thing in your life? Is it a favourite game, toy or item of clothing, or is it a person? Do the people in your life, whom you care about, know that you care? Is there something you could do to show them how important they are to you? Remember that you can tell people with words that they are important, but you can also show people very clearly that they matter, by your actions.

PRAYER

Dear God, thank you for all the things that we own and enjoy. Thank you that we have good food, beds to sleep in, toys to play with and clothes to wear. Thank you for the people who make our lives special. Please help us never to take these people for granted. Help us to show them that they are important and that we care for them. Amen

28

Welcome to everyone

Aim: To consider the importance of making everybody feel welcome.

This assembly works well at the start of a new school year or if there are going to be visitors in school.

You will need: Three collections of 20 items in separate boxes.

The actual objects used are not important—they could be balls, pens, bags, cups, plates or jumpers—but all the items in each collection must be identical except for an 'odd one out'. For example, you might have 19 pens and one pencil; 19 tennis balls and one football; and 19 identical PE bags and one different coloured bag.

Assembly outline

Ask if any of the children remember their first day at school. Invite a few children to share how they felt. Ask if any children remember being slightly older and arriving at a new place where they didn't know anybody. Perhaps a child has recently moved schools, joined a new scout group, started attending a youth club or joined a football club. Invite some of these children to explain how they felt. Was there anyone who spoke to them? Did anyone try to make them feel welcome?

Call 20 children out to the front and, as they arrive, ask them to pick out one item each from one of your collections. (If the school is small or space is limited, simply hold up the collection, one or two items at a time, so that the children can see that most of the items are identical.) Invite the children to hold up the objects so that the rest of the school can see them.

Ask the audience what they notice about the items. It is likely that the first answer will be that one of the 20 is different. Encourage the children to imagine that that item (ball, bag or pencil) had feelings. How do they think it might be feeling at the moment—lonely, sad, odd-one-out, frightened, embarrassed or scared? Ask the children to return their items to the box, pick out an object each from another collection and hold it up. Repeat the sequence above, asking how the 'different' item would feel. Do the same with the third collection of 20 objects.

When the children have sat down, explain that some-times all of us can feel left out of things. It is likely that, at some point in our lives, we will all feel like the odd one out. It may be that we arrive at a new place where we don't know anyone else. It may be that we feel as if we are the only person in the class who can't do their maths. Perhaps we feel as if we are the only person on a sports team who can't play football, catch or hit the ball. Feeling as if we are the odd one out is not pleasant.

Invite a number of children to come to the front. Without embarrassing any of them by pointing out individual features, simply ask the other children which of the volunteers are exactly the same. Obviously none of the children will be identical. (If you have identical twins or triplets in the school, you may like to prearrange for them to tell the others how they are different from each other. These differences may be subtle, but they will be there.) Remind the children that the fact that we are all different adds a wonderful variety to the world. However, sometimes, feeling different and feeling that we don't fit in can make us very sad.

Explain that all of us have a part to play in making people feel welcome or part of the community, whether at school, at home or in after-school clubs, scout groups or sports clubs. Remind the children about one of the collections you showed them earlier—for example, the balls. Ask them to imagine that they are the odd one out in a situation. What would they like people to do to make them feel welcome or part of the group? Answers may include talking to them, standing with them, inviting them to play, sitting next to them or even simply smiling at them.

Point out that sometimes it is difficult to make people welcome, because it means that we have to choose to stop doing something we want to do and take the time to help another person. For example, if all our friends are playing football and we see a new child standing on their own, it is difficult to decide to stop playing the game and go and ask the new person if they would like to play. However, the consequence of our action will not only be that the new person feels happy and welcome, but that we also feel good about our decision and may make a new friend.

Challenge the children to make a special effort this week to look out for people who are on their own or are visiting the school. Challenge them to be especially welcoming.

What the Bible says

The Bible encourages us to think of other people and their needs as more important than our own. **Philippians 2:3–4** encourages us not only to think about ourselves and our own interests, but also to think about what is best for those around us.

Luke 10:25–37 tells the story of the good Samaritan. (If the children are not familiar with it, you may wish to tell it briefly.) In this story it is the person who is not expected to help the injured man who actually takes the time to stop and care for him. Sometimes it can be the unexpected people who are good at thinking about others and making them feel welcome.

Pause for thought

Can you think of a time when you felt like the odd one out? Can you think of a time when you felt lonely or sad? Did anyone help you in that situation? If so, how did they help and how did that make you feel? It isn't pleasant to feel left out and lonely, and all of us are able to stop other people feeling this way. Let's make a special effort this week to be on the look-out for people who are alone or seem left out or sad. Let's make the decision to include people and make school a happier place to be.

PRAYER

Dear God, thank you for all our friends. Please help us to be sensitive to other people's needs. Help us to notice when people are sad, lonely or feeling left out, and please help us to take time to include them and make them feel welcome. Amen

29

When things go wrong

Aim: To consider that almost everything we do affects another person in some way. Our actions can either add to their difficulties or can help them.

You will need: Two Jenga games or sets of blocks that can be built into two towers.

Giant Jenga blocks are effective but care must be taken to ensure safety.

Assembly outline

With the children watching, set up two towers of blocks on separate table tops. Ask the children what would happen if you knocked one of the tables as you walked past. Demonstrate by nudging the table and causing the tower to topple.

Explain that sometimes things happen to people that make them feel as if their whole world has come tumbling down around them, just like the tower has done. Often, these are big events in people's lives, and those around them see that they are upset and treat them in a special way. For example, if a child comes into school crying one morning, a teacher will try to find out what is the matter and may explain to the other children that they need to be especially kind to that child. Because everyone knows that the child is upset for a special reason, everyone will try to be thoughtful and look after them.

However, sometimes the build-up of lots of things can make us feel very sad and can eventually make us feel as if we can't cope anymore.

Give a few examples of situations that could make the children feel sad or let down, and, as you explain each one, carefully remove some bricks from the second tower. For example, someone might not let another child play with them in the playground and it can make that child feel sad. (Carefully remove one of the blocks.) Someone may have been shouted at by their mum before they came to school and they could be feeling unhappy. (Remove another block.) Someone might have had an argument with their friend... someone might have a sick pet... someone might have heard that people were talking about them behind their backs and so on. Ask the children to give their own examples and, as they suggest things that could make them feel down in the dumps, remove another block (or ask the children to do so).

Point out that, just as we can remove all these blocks and the tower will stay standing, all the little things that have made us feel a bit sad, worried or hurt can add up, but we can still look as if we are OK on the outside. This means that no one knows how unhappy we are feeling.

Give a couple more examples, making sure that the tower now collapses. Explain that eventually it can be something little that suddenly makes us feel we can't cope any more. When this happens, we might get very angry or very sad or we just want to move away from everybody because we are scared that they will hurt us again.

It may seem to be a very small thing that 'pushes us over the edge' but really it is the build-up of lots and lots of little problems.

Explain to the children that, because we can't see what others are feeling on the inside and often have no idea what problems they are facing, it is very important to try to be sensitive to people all of the time. It is important to stop and think before we speak and before we take certain actions.

Challenge the children to think about the way they behave towards others. Encourage them always to think before they speak. Point out that the way a person is feeling affects the way they behave at the time. If a person is feeling happy when someone says they can't join in a particular game, they may happily go off and join in with others. However, if that same child is already feeling sad when they are told that they cannot join in, they may be very upset.

Encourage children who are feeling as if things are getting on top of them to talk to a member of staff today.

What the Bible says

Sometimes we feel badly let down and hurt by the people around us. Sometimes we feel unable to cope with the situations in which we find ourselves. When this happens, we can feel very sad and alone. Sometimes we let other people down ourselves, and this can also make us sad and lonely. The Bible tells us that whatever we have done and however sad and lonely we feel, God is always there. **Joshua 1:9** says, 'God will be with you wherever you go.'

Pause for thought

Think for a moment about the people seated around you. Some of them will be good friends of yours, but some of them you will hardly know at all. Take a moment to realise that any of these people could be feeling sad or could be facing problems at school or at home, or could be particularly tired and down in the dumps today. Even if each of them is feeling wonderfully happy, the way you treat them will make a huge difference to their day.

Do you feel sad, lonely or frightened today? If you do, maybe you should talk to a member of staff about it, because they may be able to help you.

PRAYER

Dear God, thank you for each person in this school. Thank you that even though we may not know what is happening in each person's life, you do know and you care. Please help us to think about others today. Help us to be thoughtful and sensitive to those around us. Amen

30

Who can you trust?

Aim: To consider the people in our lives whom we can truly trust and the importance of showing others that we can be trusted.

You will need: Two people (children or adults) who will answer questions from the front; four appropriate questions to ask them.

It works well if your two volunteers are one child and one adult, especially if it is the child who gets the answers correct. You could decide to use eight volunteers—a different pair to answer each question.

The people in each pair need to be known to have very different interests, so that the audience would expect (trust) a definite person to know the answer to the question asked. Before the assembly, each pair should be secretly told how to answer the question they will be asked, making sure that the person least likely to know the answer answers it correctly. There needs to be an element of surprise for the audience. For example, if you have a volunteer who is mad keen on football, make sure it is their unlikely partner who gives the correct score in the football question.

The questions might be:

- What was the score of the Brazil v Croatia match in the World Cup in 2014? (Answer: 3–1)
- Who wrote the book *Pride and Prejudice*? (Answer: Jane Austen)
- What is the capital of Austria? (Answer: Vienna)
- What was the name of the person who invented the telephone? (Answer: Alexander Graham Bell)

Assembly outline

Ask the children to think of people whom they know or might meet during a normal day—parents, teachers, friends, neighbours, shopkeepers, police, fire fighters and so on. Ask which people they think they can trust the most, and why they feel these people can be trusted.

Point out that, at some point, we all feel let down by those we trust. For example, a parent may agree to take us somewhere and then something crops up which means they can no longer do it; a friend may promise to come round to play and then, for some reason, be unable to come. If these things happen just a few times, it doesn't mean that the people concerned can't be trusted. However, if people constantly let us down or tell us lies, then we lose our trust in them.

Explain that in the 1950s there was a TV show called *Who Do You Trust?* Two people in a team each had to decide whether to trust the other person to answer a question correctly on a particular topic. Say that the children are going to play a similar game, and invite the two (or eight) volunteers to come to the front. State that the first question you are going to ask is about football. Ask the children to vote on which of the two volunteers they would trust to answer a question about football correctly. After they have voted, ask the question. React with surprise when the least expected person answers correctly. Continue in the same way with each question.

Point out that we all need to learn which people we can trust. However, alongside finding people we can trust, we also need to be people who can be trusted by others. When we are young, it may feel as if we don't have such great responsibilities as adults do. However, being trustworthy in small things is as important as being trustworthy in big things. Every job we do, every task we take part in, will affect other people in some way. If we are given a job to do, no matter how small it may seem, it is important to do it to the best of our ability.

Explain that if someone does a small task well, they are much more likely to be given a bigger responsibility in the future. For example, if a teacher leaves two friends sharpening pencils in the classroom for a few minutes and returns to find them messing around, the teacher is less likely to give them a more important job in the future. However, if the teacher finds them sharpening pencils sensibly, the teacher will realise that they can be trusted with a small job and will be likely to trust them with greater responsibility at a later date.

(You may want to include the issue of 'stranger danger' here, giving the children a number of scenarios and asking them who they would trust in each situation. For example, if they got separated from a parent in the town centre, who would they ask to help them? If they got lost in a supermarket, who would they trust?)

What the Bible says

The Bible says a lot about trust. It encourages us to trust in God and also to be people who will always tell the truth and keep our promises—people who can always be trusted. **Luke 16:10** says, 'Whoever can be trusted with very little can also be trusted with much.' This verse makes it clear that the little things we do are very important if we are to be trusted with bigger responsibilities in the future.

PRAYER

Dear God, please help us to be people who can be trusted. Help us to try our best in everything, help us to be good friends and help us to tell the truth. Thank you for the people whom we know we can trust. [Ask the children to think quietly about those people for a moment.] Amen

Christian calendar events

3I

Advent

Aim: To consider that Advent is a time for waiting and preparation, as Christmas is on its way.

You will need: Volunteer 'actors' as follows:
- A seated child holding a toothbrush and looking bored (in the dentist's waiting room)
- A child peering up and down the road, standing on one leg then another, looking frustrated (waiting for a bus)
- A child holding an armful of shopping, looking cross and sighing a lot (waiting at a checkout)
- A child holding a Christmas stocking, jumping up and down and looking excited (waiting for Christmas Day)
- A child rubbing their tummy, rolling their eyes and holding a knife and fork (waiting for food)
- A child dressed in nativity-style clothes and holding a Bible
- A staff member to arrive at the assembly later than everyone else

An Advent calendar, an Advent candle, an Advent wreath or a downloaded picture of an Advent wreath (all optional).

Before the assembly, make sure that the children involved know where they will stand when you invite them to the front. The child with the Bible needs to be positioned at the end of the line of waiting children.

Assembly outline

Once all the children are seated, move to the front of the room and carry out actions that suggest that you are waiting for something (folding your arms, peering towards the door, sighing, tapping your foot and looking at the clock). Continue to do this until the latecomer arrives, and then comment on the fact that you have been waiting for them. Ask the children if they have ever had to wait a long time for anything.

Explain that some volunteers are going to come to the front and pretend they are waiting for something. You want the rest of the children to guess what they are waiting for.

Invite your volunteers to stand in a line and carry out their actions, one after another. Give the seated children a short time to watch all the volunteers, and then work your way along the line, asking what they think each child is waiting for. As each situation is guessed correctly, comment on how frustrating it can be to wait for a long time in the dentist's or doctor's surgery, at a bus stop or a checkout or for dinner to be ready.

The situations will be straightforward for the children to guess until you come to the final child, in nativity-style costume. Explain that this child is holding a Bible in which we read about the Christmas story. Jewish people believe that, thousands of years ago, God promised to send a special person to earth one day, called the Messiah. Tell the children that the Bible has two parts to it, called the Old and New Testaments. In the Old Testament, there are lots of writings describing this Messiah. The Jewish people had waited and waited for the Messiah to arrive, and Christians believe that Jesus was the Messiah whom the Jewish people had been waiting for.

Show the children the Advent calendar, candle and/or wreath. Explain that when we arrive at 1 December, we feel excited because we can start to open our Advent calendars. We often think of Advent as being a countdown to Christmas Day. Although this is true, the season of Advent began as a time set aside for people to prepare themselves to celebrate the birth of Jesus. Christians believe that the birth of Jesus was so important that they want to take time to think about it and remember how amazing it is.

If an Advent wreath is available, explain that each of the five candles in the wreath has a special meaning. When used in church, one candle in the wreath is lit on each of the Sundays leading up to Christmas Day. The first and second candles are purple and represent hope and love. The third candle is pink and represents joy. The fourth candle is purple and represents peace. The final candle, which is placed in the centre of the wreath, is white and represents the Christian belief that Jesus is central to Christmas and is the 'light of the world'.

What the Bible says

The Old Testament part of the Bible records many prophecies that speak about the coming of the Messiah. These are just a few of them:

- **Isaiah 9:6–7:** 'For to us a child is born, to us a son is given, and the government will be on his shoulders. And he will be called Wonderful Counsellor, Mighty God, Everlasting Father, Prince of Peace. Of the greatness of his government and peace there will be no end.'
- **Isaiah 7:14:** 'Therefore the Lord himself will give you a sign: the virgin will conceive and give birth to a son, and will call him Immanuel.'
- **Micah 5:2:** 'But you, Bethlehem Ephrathah, though you are small among the clans of Judah, out of you will come for me one who will be ruler over Israel.'

Christians believe that these and many other prophecies came true when Jesus was born.

Pause for thought

Most people don't like waiting. Many of us feel impatient when we have to wait for something to happen, especially if it is something exciting. However, the time of Advent not only gives us a chance to get excited about Christmas, put up decorations and wrap presents; it also gives us the opportunity to think about how Christmas began 2000 years ago, when baby Jesus was born. Are our minds so full of excitement about Christmas that we forget about the things that really matter, such as love, joy and peace?

PRAYER

Dear God, thank you for the excitement of Christmas. Thank you for the decorations, parties, presents and everything that we enjoy. In all the excitement, please help us not to forget that the most important things in life can't be bought with money. Please help us to remember the true meaning of Christmas. Amen

32

Christmas

Aim: To consider the true meaning of Christmas and where it all began.

You will need: Four boxes of different shapes and sizes, wrapped in Christmas paper, with different contents, as follows:

- Box 1: Christmas decorations, such as tinsel, a small tree, baubles or lights
- Box 2: a few wrapped presents (sweets, pencils or anything cheap)
- Box 3: party blowers, balloons or crackers
- Box 4: the story below, on a folded piece of paper, or a picture book telling the Christmas story

When many people think about Christmas, they think of decorations, Christmas trees, presents, parties and all sorts of exciting things. However, many people fail to think about how Christmas began. So let's stop for a moment and think about the real reason that we celebrate Christmas.

Over 2000 years ago, an angel appeared to a woman called Mary. The angel told Mary that she was going to have a very special baby. The baby's name would be Jesus and he was going to change the world.

Mary and her husband Joseph had to travel to a town called Bethlehem because of an order from the Roman emperor that each person should return to the town where they had been born so that all the people could be counted. When Mary and Joseph arrived in Bethlehem, the town was already full of people and, as all the places to stay were full, Mary and Joseph were allowed to sleep in a stable. It was here that baby Jesus was born.

In the middle of the night, some shepherds arrived at the stable to see baby Jesus. They told Mary and Joseph that they had been out on the hills looking after their sheep when suddenly angels had appeared in the sky and told them that a special baby had been born. As soon as the angels had left, the shepherds had hurried to find the baby.

Later, some wise men came to visit baby Jesus. They had seen a special star in the sky and followed it all the way to Bethlehem.

Christians believe that baby Jesus was God's special gift to the world. Jesus grew up to change the world. It is because of him that we have Christmas, but so often he is forgotten in all of the excitement.

Assembly outline

At the start of the assembly, the boxes should be hidden from view.

Ask the children if they are feeling excited as they think about Christmas approaching. Ask what they enjoy most about Christmas and what they are looking forward to most this year. At some point, a child will mention presents.

Announce that you have brought some presents to the assembly and uncover them.

Invite a volunteer to open the first present. When the child pulls out the decorations, explain that many people enjoy decorating their homes at Christmas. Many people enjoy seeing all the Christmas lights appear and the beautiful displays in the shops.

Ask a few children to come to the front to hold the decorations while another volunteer opens the second present. Invite more children to the front to hold (or open) the small gifts contained inside Box 2. Explain that, for many people, the main excitement of Christmas is about the presents that they receive.

Call another volunteer to open Box 3. Invite a few children to the front to blow the party blowers or pull the crackers. Explain that, for many people, the best part of Christmas is meeting up with family and friends and having a good time together.

Ask someone to open the fourth present. When this volunteer pulls out the folded story (or Christmas story book), ask the children at the front to sit down.

Explain that putting up decorations, giving and receiving presents and having parties are all wonderful parts of Christmas, but that in this box there is a message about how all the excitement first began.

Read out the story from the piece of paper or book.

Remind the children that, in all the excitement of Christmas, it's important to pause sometimes, think about how it all began and remember the true meaning of Christmas.

What the Bible says

The Bible records the birth of Jesus in **Luke 1:26—2:20** and **Matthew 1:18—2:12**. You may like to ask a child to read parts of these passages during the assembly. For example, Luke 2:1–19 tells the story of Jesus' birth in the stable and the visit from the shepherds.

Pause for thought

Close your eyes and think about your favourite parts of Christmas. Think about the decorations that you put up in your home or that you see when you visit the shops. Think about Christmas morning and the excitement of receiving gifts. Think about all the people you will see at Christmas and the excitement of playing together and having a good time. Now take a moment to think about how it all began— in a poor stable with the birth of a baby. He wasn't rich. He didn't even have a proper place to sleep: he was placed in a trough that the animals would eat from. However, he grew up to change the world.

PRAYER

Dear God, thank you for the excitement of Christmas. Thank you for all the things that we enjoy so much. In the activities of Christmas, please help us to remember that it all began with the birth of baby Jesus. Amen

33

Lent

Aim: To consider that Lent is a preparation time, as Easter is on its way.

You will need: Objects to illustrate situations that need preparation, if they are to be successful. For example:

- a suitcase (holiday)
- an exam paper (taking an exam)
- a football (football match)
- an invitation, wedding dress, or wedding photo (wedding)
- a stocking (Christmas)
- a knife and fork (a meal)

Assembly outline

Ask the children what time they got out of bed this morning. When they volunteer their answers, appear surprised that they didn't simply jump out of bed and run straight to school. Ask them why this would not be possible.

When they point out that they had to get ready, invite them to tell you all the things they needed to do before coming to school. The obvious answers will include getting up, having breakfast, packing their bag and having a wash. However, encourage them to think more widely, to include preparations made many days or weeks before. Examples could be buying their breakfast cereal from a shop, buying school uniform, or even applying to the school years earlier. In fact, a great deal of preparation has gone into their arrival at school this morning.

Tell the children that you are going to show them a number of objects and you want them to think about what situation each item could illustrate. Show each item in turn. Encourage them to name the item, suggest what situation it illustrates and then list all the preparation needed before that event occurs.

For example, show the football, which illustrates a football match. Before the match can happen, it is likely that both teams will have been practising football for many years. They will have been bought footballs, football kits and boots. They may have attended a football club in school or elsewhere. Moving forward in time, someone will have needed to take time to arrange the match and someone will have been prepared to drive the players to the ground.

Show the suitcase, to illustrate going on holiday. Some-one will have worked hard to earn money to pay for the holiday; the holiday will have been booked; flights may have been arranged; clothes will have been washed, pass-ports checked, sun cream bought and so on.

For any of the situations listed above, a great deal of preparation is needed.

Ask the children what would happen if no preparation had been made for any of these situations. Explain that if a student doesn't prepare for an exam, they are not able to do well in it. If preparations for Christmas are not made, there will be no tree, no decorations and no presents. In fact, if people made no preparations, most things would not happen at all or would be very disappointing. Point out that most of the important things in life need preparation of some kind.

Explain that Lent is the time of preparation for Easter, just as Advent is the time of preparation for Christmas. Christians believe that it is good to stop and focus their minds on God as they get ready to celebrate the most important events in the Christian calendar—the death and resurrection of Jesus.

At Christmas we remember that Jesus was born in Bethlehem. We know very little about his life for the next 30 years, but, at the age of 30, he was ready to begin telling people about God and performing amazing miracles. Jesus knew that the next few years of his life were going to be very busy and often difficult, and so, before he began this work, he spent 40 days in the desert getting prepared. After 40 days, he left the desert, ready for the work ahead. For this reason, the period of Lent lasts for 40 days, starting on Ash Wednesday (the day after Shrove Tuesday, when pancakes are traditionally made) and finishing on Easter Day. (Note that the 40 days of Lent do not include Sundays.)

During the 40 days that Jesus spent in the desert, he fasted, which means that he went without food. For this reason, Christians sometimes give something up during Lent. They may decide not to watch television, not to eat chocolate and so on. The idea is that this helps them to think about God more. However, more recently there has been a move to do something positive during Lent rather than give something up. People may decide to do a kind deed every day during Lent, such as making a cake for a neighbour, sending someone a card or making their own bed.

Challenge the children that, even if they don't celebrate Lent themselves, they could still make a decision to do something special for someone every day and see what a difference it makes.

What the Bible says

The story of Jesus' time in the desert is found in **Matthew 4:1–11** and **Luke 4:1–13**. As Christians move through Lent, many like to read the story of Jesus' journey towards Jerusalem, where he would eventually die and come back to life. In **Luke 9:51** we read that 'Jesus resolutely set out for Jerusalem'. The subsequent chapters record his journey, culminating in his death (**Luke 23:44–49**) and his resurrection (**Luke 24:1–12**). As he made this journey, he stopped many times on the way to spend time with people and heal them. Christians believe that just as Jesus showed love and care to the people he met, so they should show love and care to those around them.

Pause for thought

The season of Lent is a good time to stop and think about our own lives. Maybe you would like to use this time as a challenge to do something positive and special in the lead-up to Easter. You could make your bed each day, or decide to say something kind to someone every day, or read your younger sibling a story each night. Lent is a time to think about other people more than we think about ourselves. Is there something you could do to show others that you care about them?

PRAYER
Dear God, thank you for the celebration of Easter. Please help us to use this time of Lent to think about other people and to show them that we care. Amen

34

Easter

Aim: To look at the Easter story and consider its meaning for Christians throughout the world.

You will need: An Easter egg in a cuboid box; scissors; sticky tape.

Before the assembly, carefully undo the box and remove the Easter egg. Remove any contents from the egg itself.

Unfold the box and cut it so that it forms the shape of a cross, as shown below.

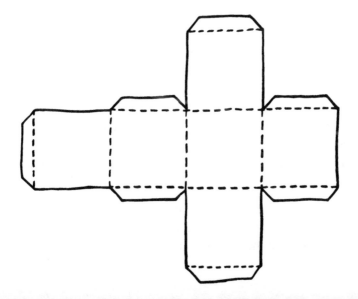

Refold the box and stick the sides together with tape so that it looks as if it hasn't been opened. Use as little tape as possible, so that it is easy to undo during the assembly. Replace the egg in the box and seal it. The box will look slightly different from before, but this should not be obvious to the children.

Assembly outline

Ask the children what is special about the time of the year. They will give a variety of answers, including spring, school holidays and Easter. Ask them what they like best about Easter: at some point, you will get the answer 'Easter eggs'. Explain that you have brought an Easter egg to the assembly today and you want to use it to remind the children about the Easter story, which Christians around the world celebrate.

Turn the Easter egg box on its side so that it resembles a table. Explain that when Jesus was on earth, he would celebrate all the special Jewish festivals with his family or friends. Most of these events involved people gathering together to eat. Point out that Jesus' special friends are often called his 'disciples'. On one Thursday evening (now sometimes called Maundy Thursday), Jesus sat together with his disciples while they enjoyed a special meal called the Passover. After the meal, Jesus and the disciples went out for a walk, and Jesus was arrested by some soldiers, even though he had done nothing wrong.

On the following day, known as 'Good Friday', Jesus was crucified on a cross. Open the box, place the egg to one side, undo the sticky tape and show the children the cross.

Explain that once Jesus had died, a rich man called Joseph came and put his body in a tomb that had been cut into rock, probably looking like a small cave. To seal the tomb, a huge, heavy stone was rolled in front of it. Point out that the shape of the Easter egg is symbolic of the large stone.

Tell how, on Sunday morning, some women came to visit the tomb and had an enormous surprise. The huge stone had been moved to one side and the tomb was open. More than that, an angel appeared to the women and told them that Jesus was not there any more because he was alive again. When the women heard this news, they ran back to the room where the rest of Jesus' disciples were waiting. When two of the disciples, called Peter and John, heard what the women said, they ran to the tomb and looked inside. As the women had said, the tomb was empty; Jesus had risen from the dead!

Open the Easter egg and show the children that it is empty. Explain that the empty egg reminds us that Jesus' tomb was empty—and he is alive today.

Say that, after this event, Jesus went to visit his friends to show them that he was alive again.

For Christians, Easter is a very special celebration of the death and resurrection of Jesus.

What the Bible says

The story of the resurrection of Jesus is found in all four Gospels: **Matthew 28:1–15**; **Mark 16:1–8**; **Luke 24:1–49** and **John 20:1–29**. In each of these Gospels, the writers tell us different details about Jesus coming back to life. The story in this assembly is mainly based on the account in Luke 24. It may be suitable for a child to read part of this account out loud as part of the assembly.

Pause for thought

The thought of Jesus dying may not seem like a happy one. However, Christians believe that Easter is a wonderful celebration because Jesus is no longer dead, but is alive for ever. Christians see the Easter story as one full of hope and joy. They believe that Jesus' death opened up a way for people to be forgiven by God for anything wrong that they have done. They also believe that Jesus is now in heaven and, because he is alive, he can always be close to us and hear us if we ever talk to him.

PRAYER
Dear God, thank you for the Easter story and the hope that it brings to us. Thank you that Jesus is no longer dead but that he is in heaven and is alive for ever. Thank you that we can talk to him at any time and he will always listen to us. Amen

35

Pentecost

Aim: To consider Pentecost as the beginning of the Christian church and to see that the 'flame' of Christianity has continued to burn throughout the years.

You will need: A birthday cake with candles that can be blown out completely; birthday candles that relight after being blown out.

Assembly outline

Ask the children if they have any favourite days during the year. Ask why they like those particular days and what happens on those days to make them special. No doubt someone will mention birthdays; when they do, ask if any of the children have traditions that take place on their birthdays, such as parties, meals out, presents or cakes.

Invite any of the children who have a birthday today to come to the front. (If no one has a birthday today, find the child with the closest birthday.) Show everyone the birthday cake and light the candles. Ask them to join you in singing to the birthday children, and allow these children to blow out the candles.

Explain that the Christian church has a special celebration each year to remember its birthday. The celebration is called Pentecost and the flames of the birthday candles remind us what happened on the first Pentecost.

The story of Pentecost can be found in the Bible, in **Acts 2:1–13**. Explain that Jesus' followers, the disciples, were frightened and sad because Jesus had gone back to heaven and they didn't know what to do next. They were all together in a locked room when suddenly there was a sound like a rushing wind, and little flames of fire appeared and came to rest on each of them. Suddenly they all felt different. They realised that God had kept his promise and sent the Holy Spirit to live in them. From then on, the disciples went out and told everyone they met about Jesus, and the Christian church began to grow.

Remove the candles from the cake and replace them with the relighting candles. Ask a different child to come to the front. Light the candles and ask the child to blow them out. When the candles relight themselves, ask another child to blow them out. Repeat this a few times and, while the candles are still burning, explain that Christians believe that God's light will never go out. Even though sometimes people may try to stop others from being Christians or believing in God, the light of God's love will never be completely extinguished.

The celebration of Pentecost takes place 50 days after Easter, with Easter Day counted as the first day.

What the Bible says

After Jesus had risen back to life, he spent the next 40 days appearing to many different people. On one of these occasions, he told his disciples to stay in Jerusalem and wait until God sent them the special gift of the Holy Spirit, as he had promised (**Acts 1:4**). On another occasion he went with his disciples to the Mount of Olives. Here he said his final words to the disciples: 'You will receive power when the Holy Spirit comes on you; and you will be my witnesses in Jerusalem, and in all Judea and Samaria, and to the ends of the earth' (**Acts 1:8**).

When Jesus had said these words, he was taken up into heaven and the disciples went to a room to wait for God to keep his promise. Ten days later, Pentecost happened.

Pause for thought

The disciples were sad when Jesus went back to heaven. For a while they probably felt very lonely. Have you ever felt lonely? Have you ever thought that no one really understands how you feel? Think for a moment about the candles that could not be blown out. Christians believe that God's love goes on for ever and will never end. Think about the people who love you. Could you do something today to help someone else feel loved? When we love other people, the flame of love is passed on to them.

PRAYER

Dear God, thank you that you are always there beside me. Thank you for all those people who love me. Please help me to show love for other people, so that the flame of love can burn brighter in all of our hearts. Amen

National days

This short series looks at the patron saints of England, Ireland, Scotland and Wales.

The assemblies can be used for information or as part of a commemoration of the special days:

St Andrew's Day
Scotland,
celebrated 30 November

St David's Day
Wales,
celebrated 1 March

St George's Day
England,
celebrated 23 April

St Patrick's Day
Ireland,
celebrated 17 March

36

St Andrew's Day: being a friend

Aim: To consider the origins of St Andrew's Day (patron saint of Scotland) and the lessons that can be learnt from his life.

You will need: A piece of blue paper with a white diagonal cross on it (the flag of St Andrew); a map of the British Isles (England, Scotland, Wales and Ireland); a Union Jack.

Assembly outline

Show the children the blue and white flag and ask if they have seen it before and if they can tell you anything about it. Explain that it is called the flag of St Andrew and is the national flag of Scotland.

Say that today you are going to be thinking about the man after whom the blue and white flag is named. Show the children the Union Jack and ask them to locate St Andrew's cross on it.

If this assembly is being used to tie in with St Andrew's Day (30 November), draw the children's attention to the date and ask them if they know what special occasion it represents. Ask if they have any idea who St Andrew is and explain that he is known as the patron saint of Scotland.

A saint is someone who has died but has had a big impact on the world and who some people believe can still have a guiding or protecting influence on the world today. Patron saints are often regarded as the special guardians of specific countries, although they can also be considered as the specific protectors of different organisations, individuals or trades. Point out the four countries that make up the British Isles on the map and explain that each country has its own patron saint.

There are some historical facts that we know about St Andrew. He is the odd one out among the patron saints of England, Ireland and Wales, because he actually lived during the time of Jesus. The Gospel of John tells us that Andrew was possibly the first of the disciples to follow Jesus. As soon as Andrew had talked with Jesus, he introduced Jesus to his brother, who was called Peter. Both Peter and Andrew were fishermen and both became part of Jesus' group of twelve disciples.

Later, Peter became the leader of the church, but we don't read a lot about Andrew. One of the Bible stories in which Andrew does feature is the feeding of the 5000 (**John 6:1–13**). Jesus spoke to a huge crowd of people for the whole day, and then he told the disciples to feed them all. Although the disciples said that it was impossible to feed so many, Andrew brought a little boy to Jesus who offered up his five loaves and two fish. Jesus performed a miracle, using this small amount of food to feed the whole crowd.

After Jesus had gone back to heaven, Andrew travelled around, telling people about Jesus. Eventually he was killed for following Jesus. Andrew refused to be crucified in the same way as Jesus had been, as he felt that Jesus was much more important than he was. So it is thought that Andrew was crucified on a diagonal cross. This is the reason for the cross on St Andrew's flag.

Point out that, although we know little about St Andrew's life, it seems that he was a man who cared about people and spent his life trying to help them. It is interesting that Andrew became a follower of Jesus before his brother Peter, and yet Peter became the leader of the disciples. We don't read that Andrew was jealous in any way. It seems that he was willing to stay in the background and simply introduce others to Jesus.

Explain that some people are declared 'saints' or are considered to be important because of big things that they have done. However, most are simply people who have gone out of their way to stand up for what they believe to be right and to care for others.

What the Bible says

References to Andrew's life are found in the Bible at:

- **John 1:40–42:** Andrew's first meeting with Jesus
- **Matthew 4:18** and **Mark 1:16:** Andrew the fisherman
- **Mark 1:29:** Andrew's home
- **Mark 3:18** and **Luke 6:14:** Andrew in the list of disciples
- **Mark 13:3:** Andrew asking questions of Jesus

- **John 6:8–9:** the feeding of the 5000
- **John 12:20–22:** Andrew introducing people to Jesus
- **Acts1:13:** after Jesus' ascension

Pause for thought

Have you ever felt jealous? Have you ever felt that someone was given a privilege or responsibility that should have been given to you? St Andrew is a great example of someone who was willing to stay in the background. He wasn't always noticed by everyone but he had a big enough effect on the world to be remembered more than 2000 years later.

PRAYER

Dear God, thank you for people who are good examples to us. Thank you for the life of St Andrew. Thank you that even though it seemed that other people were given more important jobs than he was, he didn't complain but instead continued to help people and do what he believed to be right. Amen

37

St David's Day: doing the little things

Aim: To consider the origins of St David's Day (patron saint of Wales) and the lessons that can be learnt from his life.

You will need: A daffodil; a leek; a piece of black paper with a yellow cross on it (the flag of St David); a picture of the Welsh flag (green and white with a red dragon); map of the British Isles.

Assembly outline

Show the children the black and yellow flag and ask if they have seen it before and if they can tell you anything about it. Explain that it is called the flag of St David and is often used to represent Wales. Show the alternative white and green flag with a dragon on it and explain that this is the more frequently used Welsh flag.

Say that today you are going to be thinking about the man after whom the black and yellow flag is named.

If the assembly is being used to tie in with St David's Day (1 March), draw the children's attention to the date and ask if they know what special occasion it represents. Ask if they have any idea who St David is, and explain that he is known as the patron saint of Wales.

A saint is someone who has died but has had a big impact on the world and who some people believe can still have a guiding or protecting influence on the world today. Patron saints are often regarded as the special guardians of specific countries, although they can also be considered as the specific protectors of different organisations, individuals or trades. Point out the four countries that make up the British Isles on the map and explain that each country has its own patron saint.

There are some historical facts that we know about St David (or 'Dewi Sant', as he is known in Wales). He lived in the sixth century and died on 1 March 589, which is why St David's Day is celebrated on that date. It is said that he was over 100 years old when he died.

David was educated in a monastery and later became a monk who travelled around telling people about God. He spent most of his time travelling around Wales, setting up churches and caring for people, but it is thought that he also visited England, France and even Jerusalem. He became an archbishop, one of the leaders of the church.

David eventually settled down to live in West Wales, where he founded a monastery. He lived a very simple life, eating bread and vegetables that the monks grew in their gardens, keeping bees for honey and providing the poor and needy with clothes and food. St David's cathedral can still be visited in the city of St David in West Wales.

On St David's Day, people in Wales wear a national emblem to remind them of David. Ask the children if they know what these national emblems are. Show them the daffodil and the leek. Explain that each country has a flower as its national emblem (a rose for England, a thistle for Scotland, a daffodil for Wales and a shamrock for Northern Ireland). Ask the children if they can guess why the leek should be a Welsh national emblem. The story is told that, on one occasion, the Welsh were fighting a battle against the Saxons in a field in which leeks were growing. As both the Welsh and the Saxons were dressed the same, David told the Welsh fighters to pick a leek and place it in their helmets so that they could be identified. From then on, the leek has become a national emblem of Wales.

David lived so long ago that it is difficult to distinguish between the facts and fiction of his life. However, what is certain is that he was a good, honest, caring man. The last recorded words of St David are, 'Do the little things that you have seen me do and have heard about.'

Challenge the children to think about St David's words. He realised that it is the little things that people do in their lives that make a big difference to the people around them. Ask the children if they can think of any little things that people have done for them that have helped them in some way. Maybe someone has helped them with their work, spoken to them when they were lonely or played with them when they needed a friend.

Challenge the children to copy the good things that people do. Also, challenge the children to do good things just in case people copy them.

What the Bible says

The Bible has a lot to say about the way we should live. Here are just a few of these verses, which tell us to love other people, to love our enemies and to be kind and forgiving.

- **John 13:34:** 'Love one another. As I have loved you, so you must love one another.'
- **Matthew 5:44:** 'Love your enemies and pray for those who persecute you.'
- **Ephesians 4:32:** 'Be kind and compassionate to one another, forgiving each other.'

Pause for thought

Think for a moment about a time when someone did something that helped you in some way. Maybe you were feeling down and someone came and sat with you or made you laugh. Maybe something sad had happened at home and a friend looked after you and made you feel better. In his last words, St David encouraged us to do the little things that he had done. Is there a little thing that you could do for someone today that will make their life better or happier in some way? Remember, it only needs to be something small—asking someone to play, saying thank you, helping someone, or being kind.

PRAYER

Dear God, thank you for people who are good examples to us. Please help us to copy good behaviour and to do things that will help other people in some way. Please help us to be good examples to others. Amen

38

St George's Day: standing up for what is right

Aim: To consider the origins of St George's Day (patron saint of England) and the lessons that can be learnt from his life.

You will need: A large piece of white paper or card with a *detachable* red cross made of card (see below); a map of the British Isles; a Union Jack.

Make the red cross on the flag with one of its horizontal arms extended as shown in this diagram, and folded behind. At the start of the assembly, the flag needs to be assembled and on display.

Assembly outline

Show the children the red and white flag and ask if they have seen it before and if they can tell you anything about it. Comments will probably be made about seeing the flag at sporting events. Explain that you are going to think about the flag today, considering where it came from and, especially, the man after whom it is named.

If this assembly is being used to tie in with St George's Day (23 April), draw the children's attention to the date and ask them if they know what special occasion it represents.

Explain that the red and white flag is the English flag but that it also has another name—the St George's cross. Ask the children if they have any idea who St George was. Say that he is known as the patron saint of England.

A saint is someone who has died but has had a big impact on the world and who some people believe can still have a guiding or protecting influence on the world today. Patron saints are often regarded as the special guardians of specific countries, although they can also be considered as the specific protectors of different organisations, individuals or trades. Point out the four countries that make up the British Isles on the map and explain that each country has its own patron saint.

Tell the children that, to teach them something about St George's life, you first want to remove the cross from the flag. Remove the cross and open out the extension. Hold the cross by the extended 'handle' and ask the children what it now reminds them of (a sword).

There are some historical facts that we know about St George. He was born in Turkey in the third century and, when he was old enough, he joined the Roman army. He was a good soldier and was promoted to an important rank, eventually being assigned to serve Emperor Diocletian. Show the children the 'sword' to represent George as a good soldier.

We also know that George was a Christian, which means that he was a follower of Jesus. Turn the 'sword' round to make a cross. Remind the children that the cross is a symbol of being a Christian, because Christians believe that Jesus died on a cross before he came back to life. Emperor Diocletian was a cruel emperor and he ordered George to attack other Christians, to kill them or put them in prison. When George refused, Diocletian was furious. Having been first thrown into prison, George was eventually killed. Because of George's bravery, many people began to follow the Christian religion, including the emperor's wife.

The story of how George stood up for what he believed was right and fair travelled all over the world. After he died, George became known as St George and lots of churches were built and named after him. English soldiers began to wear a red cross on their clothes or shields as a reminder of St George's bravery, and it eventually became known as St George's cross.

Say that these stories show St George to have been a brave person who stood up for what was right. Challenge the children to think about themselves. Are there times when they should be standing up for something that is right, even if it makes them unpopular? If someone is being nasty or bullying another child, do they have the courage to stand up for what is right? If someone is being dishonest and telling lies, do they have courage to stand up for truth?

Show the children the Union Jack and say that this is the flag of the British Isles. Invite the children to spot St George's cross in the flag and ask them which other countries are represented in the flag.

What the Bible says

The Bible encourages us to stand up for what is right and to speak out against things that are wrong. **Psalm 82:3–4** asks us to 'defend the weak… uphold the cause of the poor and the oppressed' and 'rescue the weak and the needy'.

In **Proverbs 31:8–9** we are told, 'Speak up for those who cannot speak for themselves, for the rights of all who are destitute. Speak up and judge fairly; defend the rights of the poor and needy.'

Isaiah 1:17 tells us, 'Learn to do right; seek justice. Defend the oppressed.' This suggests standing up for others and doing the right thing doesn't always come naturally to us, but it is something that we can practise and learn.

Pause for thought

Do you try to think about the good in other people? Do you try to stand up for what is right, or are you afraid to do so? Why not try today to stand up for people if you feel they are not being treated fairly, and tell the truth in every situation.

PRAYER

Dear God, thank you for the example of St George. Thank you that he was brave and stood up for what he believed was right. Please help us to protect other people. Help us to be brave enough to stand against bullying and unkindness. Amen

39

St Patrick's Day: forgiveness is the best way

Aim: To consider the origins of St Patrick's Day (patron saint of Ireland) and the lessons that can be learnt from his life.

You will need: A shamrock (or clover) or picture of a shamrock; a large piece of white paper with a diagonal red cross on it (the flag of St Patrick); a picture of the Irish national flag (green, white and orange vertical stripes); a map of the British Isles (optional); Union Jack (optional).

Assembly outline

Show the children the red and white flag and ask if they have seen it before and if they can tell you anything about it. Some children may think that the flag represents England. Point out that, although the English flag is also red and white, the crosses are positioned in different directions.

Explain that this flag is the flag of St Patrick and is used to represent Northern Ireland in the Union Jack. Show the children the Union Jack, if available, and ask them to locate St Patrick's cross on it. Show them the alternative green, white and orange Irish national flag.

Say that today you are going to be thinking about the man after whom the red and white flag is named.

If the assembly is being used to tie in with St Patrick's Day (17 March), draw the children's attention to the date and ask them if they know what special occasion it represents. Ask if they have any idea who St Patrick is and tell them that he is known as the patron saint of Ireland.

A saint is someone who has died but has had a big impact on the world and who some people believe can still have a guiding or protecting influence on the world today. Patron saints are often regarded as the special guardians of specific countries, although they can also be considered as the specific protectors of different organisations, individuals or trades. Point out the four countries that make up the British Isles on the map and explain that each country has its own patron saint.

There are some historical facts that we know about St Patrick. Historians are certain that he was not born in Ireland but came from a small village in England, Scotland or Wales. He was born into a rich family that owned lots of land. When he was 14 years old, some Irish raiders invaded the village and took Patrick as a slave. For six years he looked after sheep in Ireland. During this time he was sad and lonely and he began to pray in the way his parents had taught him.

During those six years, Patrick became a devout Christian. In his autobiography, he writes that after six years he heard God speak to him, telling him to walk to the coast. Patrick walked 200 miles to the east coast of Ireland, where some sailors took him across the sea and he was reunited with his parents.

Despite being happy to be home, Patrick could not forget Ireland. One day an angel appeared to him in a dream and told him to return to Ireland and tell people about God. Patrick went to college to learn more about God and to train as a minister. He then returned to Ireland and spent the next 40 years travelling throughout the country, telling the people about the Christian faith. During his lifetime thousands of people became Christians and were baptised by him.

Some people were jealous of Patrick's success and accused him of trying to make himself popular and important. This upset Patrick very much but it didn't stop him doing what he knew to be right. Towards the end of his life, Patrick wrote his autobiography. This gives us an insight into a man who was determined to tell people about God, to do the right thing and to help other people.

Show the children the shamrock, pointing out the three leaves. Explain that the shamrock is the national emblem of Ireland. It is thought that St Patrick used the shamrock, which grows all over Ireland, to explain Christian teaching about the Trinity, which says that there is only one God but he has three parts—God the Father, God the Son and God the Holy Spirit. Just as the shamrock has three parts but is one leaf, so God has three parts but is one God.

Challenge the children to think about St Patrick's life. He could have been very angry and resentful about being taken away from his family and used as a slave. He could have decided to hate the people who treated him in this way. Instead, he chose to forgive and to love the people who had wronged him. This is a great example to us. What do we do when someone hurts us? Do we hold it against them or do we forgive them?

What the Bible says

The Bible has a lot to say about forgiveness. It speaks about how much God wants to forgive us for the wrong things that we have done. The Bible explains that Jesus took the punishment for the wrong things that we have done, so God will forgive us as soon as we ask him to. **1 John 1:9** says, 'If we confess our sins, he is faithful and just and will forgive us our sins.'

The Bible also speaks about how important it is that we forgive each other. **Ephesians 4:32** says, 'Be kind and compassionate to one another, forgiving each other, just as in Christ God forgave you.'

Pause for thought

When people are unkind to us, upset us or hurt us, it is very hard to forgive them. However, when we hold bad feelings against people, it can make us feel unhappy. Are you feeling cross with someone today? Has someone done something that has made you sad or upset you? Sometimes it's good to talk to that person and explain how you feel. Sometimes it is very hard to forgive, but it is always the best way.

PRAYER

Dear God, thank you that you love us and always want to forgive us. Please help us to forgive other people, even when they hurt us. Amen

Other annual or special events

40

Education Sunday

Aim: To consider that we are fortunate to receive a good education and that many people are vital to that education.

You will need: Two simple jigsaws with the same number of pieces in each; two tables; the saying 'It takes a village to raise a child' on a large piece of paper or on screen.

The jigsaws will be completed during the assembly, so, if possible, large pieces work best. If large-piece jigsaws are not available, pieces of coloured card cut into about 15 pieces could be used.

Before the assembly, a piece should be removed from each jigsaw. If possible, remove an 'important' piece, such as one with the majority of the picture on it.

Assembly outline

Explain that today you are going to have a small competition to start the assembly. You would like six volunteers who will make up two teams of three people. Each team will take it in turns to run and collect one piece of jigsaw, bring it back to their table and put it together. As soon as a piece is placed on the table, the next team member can run to collect another. The winning team is the one that completes their jigsaw first.

You may wish to draw an imaginary line to divide the remaining children into two groups of supporters, so that they can cheer their team along. Place the two piles of jigsaw pieces an appropriate distance from the tables and, when you are ready, begin the game. As the children collect the pieces, provide a running commentary on how well the teams are doing, so that the seated children know what is happening.

There will come a point when each team begins to complain that there is a piece missing from their jigsaw. Ask them to look on the floor close to where the pieces were placed. When they can't find the missing pieces, point out that neither team can win because neither of them have completed the jigsaw, and ask them to sit down.

Explain that you actually removed the pieces before the start of the assembly because you wanted the children to think about that missing piece. A jigsaw can never be complete or whole without every part. Pick up two jigsaw pieces and describe the differences between them. One may have a flat side because it fits on the outside edge; another may have three indents and one sticking-out side. No one could say that any piece of the jigsaw is more important than another because every piece is essential.

Ask the children to think about their school and to name any adults who are part of it. You may want to record the suggestions—teachers, cook, welfare staff, bursar, school nurse and so on. Explain that just as the jigsaw needs every piece to be complete, the school needs every person to work properly and do the best they can.

Invite a volunteer to hold up the saying 'It takes a village to raise a child'. Tell the children that this saying is thought to be an old African proverb or is formed by combining a number of similar African proverbs. Ask them what they think the proverb means. Explain that the proverb suggests that it is not only their immediate family that has an effect on a child. Every person who has any contact with a child has an effect on them in some way, and children need the influence of other people if they are to grow and develop into healthy adults. The same is true for a school family. Each person in the school is involved with everyone else's life, and each person is needed.

Point out that each adult and each child in school is like a piece of the jigsaw. Each person matters; if someone is missing, it makes a difference.

If this assembly is connected to Education Sunday, explain that for more than 100 years many churches have set aside a special day each year to thank God for all those involved in education. This special Sunday is usually in February and is traditionally the ninth Sunday before Easter.

What the Bible says

Even though it was written a long time ago, the Bible speaks about the importance of teaching children. **Deuteronomy 11** speaks about the guidelines that God gave to help people live good and happy lives, and verse 19 says, 'Teach them to your children, talking about them when you sit at home and when you walk along the road, when you lie down and when you get up.' In other words, every moment of every day is a time for learning.

Pause for thought

What do you like doing most in school? What do you like doing least? Take a moment to remind yourself that even if we don't enjoy some activities as much as others, we are very privileged to be in a school that cares for us and wants us to learn. Pause to remember that many children in the world will never go to school and will never be able to read and write. Think for a moment about all the people who work so hard to make our school a lovely place to be. How often do we say 'thank you'?

PRAYER
Dear God, thank you for our school. Thank you for all the people who work so hard to make it a special place to be. Please help us all to remember that the way we treat one another is very important and that our actions have an impact on everyone. Amen

41

Fair trade

Aim: To consider what it means to 'be fair' in the context of Fairtrade products.

You will need: Two bags full of shopping; a bar of chocolate with 'cocoa' clearly visible in the ingredients; a table; a downloaded 'Fairtrade' label.

The first bag of shopping should contain food that has been grown or manufactured locally, such as cheese, bread, milk or meat. The second should contain Fairtrade goods that are grown, or made from products grown, overseas, such as bananas, sugar, nuts, tea and coffee. Your bar of chocolate should be placed in the Fairtrade bag.

As a tie-in with this assembly, you could invite a local Fairtrade representative to visit the school and run a stall selling Fairtrade products.

Assembly outline

Tell the children that you have brought your shopping with you to school today and you want to tell them about the things you have bought. Unpack the first bag, placing each item on the table so that the children can see it clearly. Give a short description of each item without stating where it originates. For example, say, 'Here I've got some cheese. I like cheese because you can use it in so many ways; I especially like cheese on toast' or 'I've bought some milk. Did you know that milk is particularly good for making our bones and teeth stronger?' Do the same with the second bag.

Invite some children to come up and look closely at both collections of food. Ask if they can spot something very different about them. The answer is that the first bag contains locally grown products, whereas the second bag contains food grown, or made from products grown, overseas. Go through all the items and explain their origins. For example, 'This cheese is made at the cheese makers down the road from milk produced at local dairy farms' and 'These bananas were grown in Columbia, which is in South America.'

Explain that farmers and manufacturers in this country expect to be paid fair prices for their products. Cheese makers have to buy milk from the dairy farmer. They then have to use the milk to make the cheese, package it, store it and send it out to the shops. All of these things cost money. When the cheese is sold, the cheese maker expects to make a profit from selling it. This should be true for people who are growing and producing food-related products all over the world. However, many people living in poorer countries have not been treated fairly. They have been paid such low wages that sometimes their families do not even have enough food to eat.

Show the children the bar of chocolate and ask if they know what ingredients are used to make it. Ask someone to read out the ingredients from the label. Explain that one of the main ingredients in chocolate is cocoa. This comes from the cocoa bean, which is grown in many poorer countries in the world. For many years, the farmers growing the cocoa beans were receiving very little money for them, even though some manufacturers in richer countries of the world were making huge amounts of money when selling the chocolate. This was and is unfair. The same is true for many products produced overseas, including coffee, tea, bananas and nuts.

Although some 'fair trading' has been going on for many years, in the 1980s a 'Fairtrade' label was developed. Show the children the label. The idea was that if any companies wanted to have the Fairtrade label on their products, they would have to show that they were paying fair prices to overseas farmers and that they were treating the farmers correctly.

The idea of Fairtrade has been so popular that now Fairtrade products are sold in all major supermarkets. Even though Fairtrade products are sometimes slightly more expensive, many people prefer to buy these products because they know that the farmers who produced the products are being treated fairly for their work.

There are now more than 1.5 million Fairtrade farmers and workers in the world. Fairtrade doesn't just include food products; there are many crafts that carry the Fairtrade label. Recently, a lot of work has been carried out by Fairtrade to ensure that people hand-stitching footballs and basketballs in factories overseas are receiving a fair wage. Many balls now carry the Fairtrade label.

Encourage the children to look for Fairtrade products when they are in shops or supermarkets.

What the Bible says

The Bible encourages us to take care of the poor. There are many laws recorded in the Old Testament that were put in place to ensure that poor people were cared for. In **Matthew 25:31–40** Jesus explains that when we help people who are hungry, thirsty, lonely, sick and poor, it is as if we were caring for him. Verse 40 says, 'Truly I tell you, whatever you did for one of the least of these brothers and sisters of mine, you did for me.'

The Bible also challenges us that if we don't help people in need, then we can't really love God. **1 John 3:17–18** says, 'If anyone has material possessions and sees a brother or sister in need but has no pity on them, how can the love of God be in that person? Dear children, let us not love with words or speech but with actions and in truth.'

Pause for thought

Pause for a moment and think about your home, your bedroom, your clothes and your toys. What is your favourite food? What are you going to eat for lunch today? Remember that there are many children in the world who don't have a home and who go to bed hungry every day. Using Fairtrade products can help these children.

It is common to hear people saying that something is not fair. The next time you find yourself saying those words, why not stop and think about people who live in parts of our world where there is little housing and very little food? Let's try to do anything we can to make things better for these people.

PRAYER

Dear God, thank you for our homes, our clothes, toys and all the food that we eat each day. Please help us to do all we can to help people who have so much less than we do. Thank you for organisations like Fairtrade, which work hard to make the world a fairer and better place to live. Amen

42

Harvest

Aim: To consider our responsibility to help those who do not have enough food, using the context of the celebration of harvest.

You will need: The letters h, a, r, v, e, s, t written boldly on A4 cards; the words 'eat', 'starve' and 'share' written in large letters on pieces of card.

Muddle up the letters of the word 'harvest' before the start of the assembly. Keep the other cards covered until they are needed.

As a tie-in to this assembly, you may wish to organise a collection of food for the homeless centre or food bank in the surrounding area, or introduce a charity appeal.

Assembly outline

Invite seven volunteers to come to the front, and give each of them a card with a letter on it. (Make sure you don't give out the letters in their correct order.) Ask the children to hold the letters up so that everyone can see them clearly. If younger children are present, ask them to read each letter in turn.

Explain that the letters make up a word, and ask the seated children to look carefully and guess what the word could be. As the children guess, rearrange the card holders to show whether all the letters have been used. If no one guesses that the letters spell the word 'harvest', give the children clues, such as, 'The word I'm looking for begins with the letter "h"', 'the last letter of the word is "t"' and so on.

Once the children have guessed the word 'harvest' and the card holders are lined up in the correct order, ask the children if they know what 'harvest' means. Explain that harvest is the time when farmers gather in the crops that they have grown. In the past, when there were not many big supermarkets and much less processed food, there were huge festivals at harvest time as people thanked God that they had enough food for the coming year. Today, we are so used to going to a supermarket to buy food that it is easy to forget that much of our food is grown in fields and is harvested by farmers. It is very important that we sometimes stop and remember to be thankful for the food we have.

Encourage the children to look carefully at the word 'harvest'. Ask them if they can put any of the letters together to make other words. (Examples could be 'at', 'hat', 'vest' and so on.) After a few words have been spotted, invite the volunteers holding 'a', 'e' and 't' to step forward. Ask the seated children if they can make a word out of these three letters that has something to do with 'harvest'. Once the word 'eat' has been given, ask if anybody has a favourite food. When a few children have shared their favourites, point out how fortunate we all are to know that we will have plenty to eat today. As we approach lunch time, we may feel hungry but it will only be for a very short time.

Call for a volunteer to hold up the card with the word 'eat' written on it, and ask the children holding the letters to move back to show the word 'harvest'.

Ask the children holding 'a', 'r', 'v', 'e', 's' and 't' to step forward; then ask the seated children if they can make a word out of these six letters. You may need to give clues. Once the word 'starve' has been given, explain that although we have plenty to eat, many people in the world today do not have enough food and go to bed every night feeling hungry. Sometimes we may say that we are 'starving' but we really mean 'hungry'. In some parts of the world people really are starving and will die if they don't get any food.

Call for a volunteer to hold up the card with the word 'starve' written on it, and ask the children holding the letters to move back to show the word 'harvest'.

Ask the children holding 'h', 'a', 'r', 'e' and 's' to step forward; then ask the seated children if they can make a word out of these five letters. Once the word 'share' has been given, remind them that when we have so much food and so many other wonderful possessions, we have a responsibility to share with other people who are not as fortunate as we are. (If appropriate, tie this in to a charity collection or fundraising event.)

Call for a volunteer to hold up the card with the word 'share' written on it; then ask the children holding the letters to move back to show the word 'harvest'.

Review the assembly, pointing out that at harvest time it is good to remember how fortunate we are to have plenty to eat. It is also a good time to remember those who don't have enough to eat and to think about whether there is anything we can do to help them.

What the Bible says

The Bible tells us that God made the world and everything in it. **Psalm 24:1** says, 'The earth is the Lord's, and everything in it, the world, and all who live in it.' The Bible also speaks a great deal about God wanting people to take care of the poor and needy. **1 John 3:17–18** says, 'If anyone has material possessions and sees a brother or sister in need but has no pity on them, how can the love of God be in that person? Dear children, let us not love with words or speech but with actions and in truth.' These verses make it clear that if we say we love God, we will also care for other people.

The Bible also encourages us to be 'cheerful givers' and not to be selfish and grumpy when we give to other people (**2 Corinthians 9:7**).

Pause for thought

Have you ever felt hungry? Maybe you had to wait a bit longer than usual for your dinner or maybe you were in a rush and forgot to have breakfast. Can you remember how you felt? Unfortunately many children feel hungry day after day. Sometimes this makes them very ill and weak. Is there anything you could do to help them in some way? (If this assembly is connected to a charity event or collection, remind the children of how they can be involved.) Remember that although the problem of hunger in the world is very big, every little thing we do will help someone in some way.

PRAYER

Dear God, thank you for all the food that we eat every day. Please help those who are hungry today. Help us to be generous and to do what we can to help people with no food. Amen

43

Helping the poor: all that water

Aim: To consider the importance of water and the need to help people in other countries to receive clean water supplies.

You will need: A large empty water container; a 'lucky dip' box containing a wide selection of objects or pictures that illustrate familiar water usages (for example, bubble bath, soap, toilet roll, cup, toothbrush and so on); a flipchart; marker pens; an adult helper; downloaded pictures of children carrying water (optional).

Beforehand, arrange for a child volunteer to carry the empty water container slowly round and round the outskirts of the room throughout the assembly. The aim is to illustrate that, every day, many children walk mile after mile to collect water that isn't even safe to drink.

Your adult helper will keep count of the number of times that this child walks around the room. If possible, before the assembly, measure the distance round the room. At the end of the assembly, you can multiply this distance by the number of trips the child has made round the room, to calculate the distance walked by the child.

Assembly outline

Ask the prearranged child volunteer to come to the front, and hand them the empty container. Without explaining to the other children what is happening, tell the volunteer to set off on their journey and say that you will see them when they return. The volunteer should now begin to walk slowly round the outskirts of the room. They will continue to do this until the end of the assembly.

Invite a volunteer to describe briefly everything they have done since they got up this morning. As they do so, count in your head all the activities that required water—for example, eating breakfast, having a wash, brushing teeth, having a drink and going to the toilet. If the volunteer says that they got up late, jumped out of bed and ran straight to school, ask another child!

Explain to the children that, in the list of today's events so far, the volunteer has given some clues to the subject of the assembly. Point out that they have already used the subject for today's assembly [x] times [insert the correct number]. Repeat the activities named by your volunteer that require water usage, without indicating what the connection between the activities is.

Invite another volunteer to come forward and select an object from the lucky dip box. Ask them to hold it up and describe how the item is used. Call other volunteers to repeat this process until all the objects have been removed from the box. Ask the children if they can spot what it is that connects all the items. When they have realised that each item is used with water in some way, ask if they can think of any other ways in which we use water in our lives. If children make new suggestions, list them on a flipchart at the front.

Explain to the children that it is a great privilege to have clean, fresh, drinkable water available to us whenever we need or want it. Point out that there are many people in the world who do not have clean water and have to walk many miles to collect water every day.

Invite the volunteer who has been walking round the room throughout the assembly to come to the front. Ask the adult who has been counting the laps to calculate the total distance that has been walked. Point out that your volunteer has spent [x] minutes walking [x] miles or kilometres.

In many countries in the world, children walk much further than this in the scorching hot sun with no shade. When they eventually arrive at the water source, they fill up their container and carry it back home on their head. If possible, show some pictures of children collecting water and carrying it in this way. (You may wish to ask a volunteer to try to balance a book on their head while they walk, to demonstrate how difficult it is.) The water they collect is often dirty and the children often become sick from drinking it. Also, the water is quickly used up, which means that the children have to repeat the water collecting process day after day after day.

Tell the children that many charities work hard to provide clean water to the poorer people in the world. Many charities are providing wells and systems for cleaning dirty water supplies. Explain that we too can help by supporting these charities. If appropriate, use this opportunity to introduce a school charity event.

What the Bible says

The Bible has a lot to say about helping poorer people. **Matthew 25:35–40** records some of Jesus' words to his disciples. In this passage Jesus speaks about a time when he was hungry and thirsty, and good people gave him something to eat and drink. When the good people in the story say that they have never seen Jesus either hungry or thirsty, Jesus says, 'I tell you, whatever you did for one of the least of these brothers and sisters of mine, you did for me' (v. 40). In saying this, Jesus makes it clear that when we help the poor, we are actually helping him.

Pause for thought

Take a few moments to think about how you will use water today. Think about how lovely it is to have a cool drink on a hot day. Now imagine what it is like to walk mile after mile in the hot sun to collect water that may make you unwell if you drink it. Sometimes we find it very easy to complain about life, but actually we are very fortunate. Is there anything you could do to help these children? Why not give some suggestions to your teachers?

PRAYER

Dear God, thank you for clean, fresh water, which we drink and use every day. Please look after the people working with charities in poorer parts of the world who are trying to provide clean water for everyone. Please show us what we can do to help. Amen

44

New Year: start again

Aim: To consider that there is always the opportunity to start again.

Although this assembly is geared toward New Year, it can be easily adapted for use at any time of the year, to make the point that we always have the opportunity to start again.

You will need: Three large pieces of paper with the words 'past', 'present' and 'future' written on them; a box containing pieces of paper with different situations written on them.

Your different situations should include things that could have happened in the past, might be happening now or could happen in the future, and should be a mixture of good and bad experiences. For example:

- Past: I had a great summer holiday; I laughed at someone because they were not very good at sport; I stopped trying with my work because it was too hard; I helped my mum by tidying my bedroom.

- Present: I always try to do my best at everything; I feel sad and unhappy; I am worried about a problem that I can't tell anyone about.
- Future: I will try to do my best at everything; I will do more exercise; I will be kind to people; I will help around the house.

Assembly outline

Ask for three volunteers to hold up the large pieces of paper. Ask the children what they understand about the words 'past', 'present' and 'future'.

Show the children the box and invite a volunteer to come forward, pick a piece of paper from the box and read it out loud. Ask the children if they think the situation described on the paper refers to a past, present or future event. Tell the volunteer to move to stand next to the appropriate sign. For example, 'I stopped trying with my work because it was too hard' is a past event, so the volunteer should move to stand beside the word 'Past'.

Repeat until all the pieces of paper have been sorted into the correct categories.

Quickly reread the 'Past' events and ask the children if they can change any of those events now that they have happened. Explain that we cannot change the past. Once an action has been performed, or once words have been spoken, we cannot change it. We can, however, try to put right whatever we have done wrong.

Quickly read through the 'Present' situations. Say that perhaps we know that right now we are trying our best, being helpful, being kind and thinking about other people; if so, that is great. However, maybe we know that we are not trying our best, we are being unkind, or we are not behaving as we should. The good news is that if we realise we are not doing the right things, we can change.

Quickly read through the 'Future' events. Point out that we still have a choice about how we are going to behave and what we are going to do in the future. We cannot change the past but we can make better choices for the future.

Ask if anyone can explain what is meant by a New Year's resolution. Ask what kinds of resolutions people might make. Does anyone know someone who has made a New Year's resolution? Explain that many people see New Year as a time to make a fresh start. They decide they are going to stop doing something that they feel is bad for them or they decide to start doing something that will be good for them.

Say that although New Year is a great time to think about having a fresh start, it is not the only time when we can 'start again'. Point out that there may be things the children have done or said in the past that they feel bad about or regret. Although they can't change those things, they can say 'sorry' and try to put them right. They can also make a resolution to try not to do those things again.

You may wish to challenge the children to do something positive in the year ahead—for example, try a new sport, join a new club, try to speak to children they haven't spoken to before or make their bed each day.

What the Bible says

The Bible encourages us not to focus too much on the past but to look forward to the future. **Isaiah 43:18** says, 'Forget the former things; do not dwell on the past.' The Bible also tells us that God's love for us is new every day and will go on for ever. It tells us that nothing can separate us from God's love. **Romans 8:38–39** states that 'neither death nor life, neither angels nor demons, neither the present nor the future, nor any powers, neither height nor depth, nor anything else in all creation, will be able to separate us from the love of God that is in Christ Jesus our Lord'.

Pause for thought

We cannot change the things we have said and done in the past, but we can try to put them right if they were wrong. Is there something you wish you had never said or done? Do you need to say 'sorry' to someone? Why not do it today?

Is there something you would love to do but feel afraid to try? Maybe there is a new sport you would like to try or a new friend you would like to make. Why not choose this New Year to take the opportunities that come your way?

PRAYER

Dear God, thank you that your love for us goes on for ever. Thank you that you want to forgive our past and help us in our future. Please help us to know when to say 'sorry'. Please help us this New Year to make the most of the opportunities that are given to us. Amen

45

Remembrance Day (or Armistice Day)

Aim: To consider that we must never forget the sacrifices made for our peace.

You will need: A table; 15 objects that are large enough for the children seated at the back of the room to see clearly (for example, a book, a ball, a cuddly toy and so on); a large sheet and two adult volunteers to hold it; a large bag or bin liner; a poppy; a range of items designed to help people remember things (calendar, reminders on a mobile phone, sticky notes, diary) (optional).

Before the assembly, hide your 15 objects from view in the bag or bin liner.

Assembly outline

Ask the children to think for a moment about their earliest memory. Invite a few of them to share their memories with the other children. You may like to share one of your own earliest memories. Point out that although you have lots of lovely memories from your life, many things have also happened that you have forgotten about.

If available, show the children the collection of items designed to help people to remember things. Explain that most people use calendars or diaries to remind them of events that are going to happen. Many people also set their phones to give them reminders about things they need to do during the day. Some people leave themselves notes so that they don't forget things; some people even write reminders on their hands.

Ask the children to raise their hands if they think they have a good memory. Tell them that you are going to give them a small memory test. Invite the two adult helpers to come forward and hold the sheet between the children and the table. Remove one object at a time from the bag or bin liner. Show the object to the children and then place it on the table, behind the sheet so that the children can't see it. Repeat until all 15 items are in a line on the table.

Explain that you are going to take away the sheet for ten seconds so that the children can see all the items at once. After that, the sheet will be replaced while you remove one item from the table and place it back in the bag. The sheet will then be taken away again for ten seconds and you will ask the children to guess which item you have removed. (It is easiest if the helpers kneel down to lower the sheet, and raise it quickly by simply standing up.)

After the ten-second viewing time, remove an object. Make sure that you shuffle the remaining items along so that there is no gap in the line, as this could give the children a clue. Lower the sheet and see if the children can guess which object has been removed. Replace the removed item and repeat the process for as many times as you feel appropriate. You will find that the first few times are the most difficult for the children to guess, so you may want to reduce the amount of time you allow them to spot the missing item as the game moves on.

Point out that many of the children could not spot the missing item, even though they had seen all the items just a few moments before. We can forget things very easily. In this case, it didn't matter that the children forgot which items had been removed from the table, as it was just a game. However, there are some things that we should never forget.

Show the children the poppy. Remind them that in past years many people have been injured and many have died while fighting to bring peace to the world. Explain that at 11 o'clock on the 11th day of the 11th month (November), people stop whatever they are doing and remain silent for two minutes to remember people who have fought in wars. This was the exact date and time at which World War I ended in 1918 and it is called Armistice Day.

The poppy has become a symbol of remembrance for those who fought in World Wars I and II and in other wars since then. On the second Sunday in November, there are many ceremonies to remember those who fought in the wars, and wreaths of poppies are often placed at memorials all over the world. This day is called Remembrance Sunday.

Remind the children that since World War II there have been, and still are, other smaller wars, in which many people have been hurt and died. On this special day we also remember them.

What the Bible says

There are many wars and battles recorded in the Old Testament part of the Bible. However, Jesus tells us that he came to bring peace. The Bible says that Jesus brings us peace with God. **Romans 5:1** says, 'We have peace with God through our Lord Jesus Christ.'

The Bible also encourages us to live at peace with one another. In Romans 12:18 we read, 'If it is possible, as far as it depends on you, live at peace with everyone.'

The Bible even tells us that it is important to love our enemies and the people who hurt us. **Matthew 5:44** says, 'But I tell you, love your enemies' and **Romans 12:17** says, 'Do not repay anyone evil for evil. Be careful to do what is right in the eyes of everyone.'

Pause for thought

Let's close our eyes for a moment and say 'thank you' to God for the peace that we have in this country. Let's remember people all over the world who do not live in peace. We can pause to remember people who have been willing to give up their lives with the aim of making the world a safe and peaceful place to live in. Let's never forget their great sacrifice.

PRAYER

Dear God, thank you for the peace that we enjoy in this country. Thank you for the many people who have fought to bring that peace. Please be with those who are in the armed forces today, facing dangerous situations as they seek to bring peace. Please help us to be people who forgive and who try to love those who hurt us. Amen

46

Science Week

Aim: To remind the children of the amazing wonders of science.

You will need: The three suggested answers to each of the ten science questions below, written on separate pieces of A4 paper.

The correct answer to each question is shown in bold type for your information only.

1. **How many times does your heart beat each day?**
    50 times, 50,000 times, **100,000 times**

2. **On average, how many times does an adult blink in one minute?**
    2 times, **10 times**, 20 times

3. **Which is the largest planet in our solar system?**
    Jupiter, Mars, Earth

4. **What is the planet Mars known as?**
    Blue planet, Yellow planet, **Red planet**

5. **At what temperature does water freeze and turn to ice?**
    100°C, 10°C, **0°C**

6. **How much of the earth is covered in water?**
    10%, **70%**, 100%

7. **Which scientist is credited with inventing the telephone?**
    Alexander Bell, Alexander Fleming, Isaac Newton

8. **Which of these metals is magnetic?**
    Copper, Gold, **Iron**

9. **How many muscles do we use when we smile?**
    7, **17**, 27

10. **If humans have 7 bones in their necks, how many do giraffes have?**
    7, 12, 22

The answer papers should be sorted carefully into three piles so that each of three volunteers can show the answers to the children in the correct order.

For question 7, you may wish to point out that Alexander Fleming discovered penicillin, which is used to treat diseases, and Isaac Newton explained the idea of gravity.

Assembly outline

Ask a number of children to share which subjects they enjoy studying most at school and why they like them. Point out that we all enjoy studying different things but that every subject is important to our lives in some way.

Say that today you are going to think about the wonders of science. Explain that you are going to have a quiz in which each question relates to science in some way. There will be three suggested answers to each question, which will be held up by the three volunteers, and only one of the answers will be correct.

You may want to divide the children into two teams and appoint team leaders who will give an answer on behalf of each team. Alternatively, you may want to ask the children to choose their answers individually and keep a count of their own scores. In this case, you may wish to advise the younger children to begin with their fingers closed as fists and to lift one finger for each correct answer. You will need to ask someone to keep score if the quiz is played in two teams.

Give the children a few moments to think about each question and select their answer, before giving them the correct answer. At the end of the quiz, announce the score if it has been played as a team game.

Ask the children if they were surprised by any answers. Pick out one answer that particularly surprised you.

Say that science is an amazing subject. Through it we learn all about the world and the way things work. Some of us find it fascinating to learn about plants or animals. Others may enjoy studying electricity, finding out about materials, sound, light, forces, rocks or space. Most of us will find some aspect of science both interesting and exciting.

Over the years, scientists have worked hard to learn more and more about our world. They have discovered how to produce electricity, how to land people on the moon, how to cure many diseases and much more. Today scientists are carrying out lots of research in the hope that they will find a cure for diseases like cancer and diabetes, and even that they will be able to send people to live on the planet Mars.

People often think of scientists as extremely clever, but the truth is that they all started off as children in school. This means that there could be children listening to the assembly today who will be great scientists and will change the world in the future.

If the assembly is being used as part of a Science Week, you may wish to challenge the children to see who can find out the most unusual, amazing fact about science during the week.

What the Bible says

The Bible tells us that God is the creator of the universe and that he made everything in it. We can read the story of the creation in **Genesis 1**. Some Christians believe that it happened exactly this way. Others see it as a more imaginative account. Both sets of people still believe what it says in **Acts 17:24**: 'The God who made the world and everything in it is the Lord of heaven and earth.'

Pause for thought

We live in an amazing world. Not only are we surrounded by beautiful scenery, plants, animals and people, but we also have access to fresh water, electricity, television and technology that allows us to keep in touch with people in any country at the touch of a button. We can travel all over the world, and we are constantly finding out new things about space and the unexplored planets.

Pause for a moment to think about all the amazing discoveries that scientists have made over many years. Let's be grateful for people who work hard to produce medicines to make us better and do many other things that enhance our lives.

PRAYER

Dear God, thank you for our beautiful world and everything in it. Please help us never to take the world for granted, but always to treasure it. Thank you for scientists who work hard with the aim of making our lives even better. Amen

47

The environment matters

Aim: To consider that the world is an amazing gift that we must care for.

You will need: A large box, wrapped in bright wrapping paper with a large bow tied round it; a globe (inside the box); a collection of rubbish, some of which is recyclable (for example, plastic bottles, batteries, cans, sweet wrappers, ink cartridges and light bulbs).

Assembly outline

Invite the children to close their eyes and imagine their birthday, Christmas, a festival or special occasion when they have received a present. Ask them to think about some of the presents they have been given and to try to choose a favourite. Encourage a few of them to share what is their favourite present and why.

Ask the children how they would treat a special present. Would they leave it outside in the rain? Would they throw it around and mistreat it? Ask them how they would feel if a visitor came to their house and treated their special present in a disrespectful way.

Talk about a special gift that you have been given. If possible, make it a simple present, maybe with sentimental value, rather than a gift that cost a lot of money. Explain that because this present was special to you, you looked after it, kept it safe and treasured it.

Point out that while it is lovely to receive an expensive present, there are many things we can give to each other that do not cost any money. Ask the children if they can think of any examples (answers might include care, encouragement, love and friendship). None of these things cost money but they can make someone else feel loved, accepted and special, so they are often worth more than the things that money can buy.

Show the children the large wrapped box, and explain that inside there is a present for everybody. It is something that the children will use every day, and it is something precious. Call for a volunteer to open the present. As the child unwraps the box, tell the children that this present is free to all of them, it is important to you, and you hope that they will use the present wisely and look after it well.

When the volunteer pulls out the globe, explain that we have all been given the world as a special gift. The world is full of beauty and wonder and it is ours to enjoy and explore. It is full of a wonderful variety of people, animals and plants. It provides us with food, drink, medicine, friends, sunshine and snow, and it is an amazing place in which to live. It is a wonderful gift to be given.

Sadly, however, many people misuse the world. Ask for examples of how people do this.

Show the children the collection of rubbish and say that people throw rubbish on the floor and spoil the world's beauty. Ask the children to point out any recyclable material in the collection and explain that some people still don't recycle their rubbish, which means that more and more resources in the earth get used up and more pollution is put into the atmosphere when new products are made. Show the children the light bulb. Point out that many people don't switch off lights when they go out of a room. This may seem like a very little thing, but, if lots of people leave lights on, lots more electricity is needed. This means that more fuel is burnt to make the electricity, which means that more pollution is put into the atmosphere. When it comes to looking after our world, 'every little helps'.

Remind the children that the world is a precious gift. We have a choice whether to destroy it or treasure it. Challenge them to think about what they can do to keep the world a beautiful place in which to live.

What the Bible says

Christians believe that God made the world. **Psalm 24:1** says, 'The earth is the Lord's, and everything in it, the world, and all who live in it.' **Psalm 8** is a beautiful poem speaking about the beautiful world that God has made. **Psalm 115:16** explains that although God made the world, he has given the earth to us to care for. It says, 'The highest heavens belong to the Lord, but the earth he has given to the human race.'

Pause for thought

Close your eyes and think about something beautiful that you have seen in the world. Maybe you have been to the seaside and seen the sea stretching out in front of you, as far as you can see. Maybe you have climbed a mountain and looked down on the beautiful countryside that surrounds you. Maybe you have looked at a daisy or buttercup on the school field and seen the tiny petals and lovely colours. Take a moment to be thankful for the beauty of the world. What a challenge it is that the world is ours to care for! What can you do to care for the world?

PRAYER

Dear God, thank you for the beautiful world in which we live. Please help us all to care for it and to keep it beautiful. Amen

48

Transition: stepping stones and bridges

Aim: To consider that sometimes we need to step out to take hold of new challenges, even when it seems frightening.

This assembly is suitable for transitions between classes or schools or for encouraging the children to attempt something new.

You will need: Ten 'stepping stones' (carpet squares or A4 sheets of paper); four cones; skipping ropes; balancing beam; pictures of stepping stones in unusual places and unusual bridges (optional).

This activity works well with any number of children. For each team, you need one less 'stepping stone' than the number of people in the team.

Assembly outline

Before the assembly begins, position the cones to indicate a start and a finish line for a race.

Ask if any of the children think they are good at balancing. Explain that you want some volunteers to come to the front and see how long they can balance on one leg. As soon as they put their other foot down, they must sit down on the floor. Allow the volunteers to have a short practice to decide which is their best balancing foot. Encourage them to balance for as long as they can. You may like to continue until you have a winner or finish the game with a few winners.

Ask for twelve volunteers to form two teams of six. Line the two teams up behind the start cones and give each of the leaders carpet squares or pieces of paper. Explain that the squares represent stepping stones and you want the teams to imagine that between the start and finish lines is a river. The teams need to get all the way across the river without getting their feet wet.

This means that the leader will need to lay the first square down in front of them, step on to it, then lay down the second square and step on to that. As the leader lays down the stepping stones, the rest of the team can start to follow. At some point, children will need to share stepping stones so that the last child can pick up the square that was the first to be laid and pass it along the line so that the leader can reposition it at the front. The team that successfully transfers all its members across the water without getting their feet wet is the winner.

You may like to allow the children to have another

attempt once they have mastered the technique, or you may wish to ask a different set of twelve children to have a go.

Place the skipping ropes on the floor and invite younger children to come to the front, imagine that the ropes are very narrow bridges over water, and walk along them without falling off. Ask older children to do the same along the balancing beam.

Show the children the pictures of unusual bridges and stepping stones: there are some amazing ones to be found on the internet.

Say that sometimes we may feel frightened when we cross a bridge or walk across stepping stones. We may be scared that we will slip and end up in the water, or that the bridge will not be strong enough to hold us or that we will fall off it. Sometimes, however, we might find the prospect of crossing a bridge or stepping stones very exciting. Whatever our feelings are, we will never be able to experience what is on the other side unless we climb on to the bridge or step on to the stones.

Explain that, in the same way, we can feel frightened of moving forward into new situations in our lives. It may be that we are moving to secondary school, moving into a new class, joining a new club or trying a new activity. We may have very mixed feelings, but it is important that we find the courage to step forward. Often, when we do this, we find that things are even better on the other side.

You may like to point out that if we feel unsure about stepping out on to a bridge or stepping stone, someone may hold out their hand to help us. In the same way, if we are moving on to a new place or are trying a new activity, people will always be there to help us.

What the Bible says

The Bible tells us that God is always close to us and will never leave us. **Psalm 139:8–10** says, 'If I go up to the heavens, you are there; if I make my bed in the depths, you are there. If I rise on the wings of the dawn, if I settle on the far side of the sea, even there your hand will guide me, your right hand will hold me fast.' There are many verses in the Bible that assure us that God will be with us wherever we go.

The Bible also reminds us that not only will God be with us, but he will help us and give us strength (**Isaiah 41:10**). Alongside this, **Philippians 4:19** promises that whatever our problems may be, God will meet all of our needs.

Pause for thought

Are you worried about a new challenge that you are about to face? Remember that most people feel apprehensive about new situations. However, new experiences are a springboard into the future and the excitement that lies ahead.

PRAYER

Dear God, sometimes we feel scared when we face new situations. Please help us to have the courage to try new things. Help us to realise that you are with us in everything we do. Amen

49

Valentine's Day: love

Aim: To use Valentine's Day to remind ourselves that there are many people who love us.

This assembly about love can be used at any time of the year.

You will need: A Valentine's card; objects representing a situation which showed that someone cared about you; small pieces of different coloured card or paper, and pens (optional).

The objects you choose could be from recent events or any part of your life. It is best to use examples that you can briefly describe, such as:

- A mug (someone making you a cup of coffee)
- A picture of a hug (someone giving you a hug when you felt down in the dumps)
- A wrapped present (someone giving you a gift)
- A ball (someone inviting you to play, as a child)
- Flowers (someone buying you flowers)
- A cake (someone making you a cake when you were ill)

- A mobile phone (someone ringing you up to say 'hello')
- A homemade card (a child making a 'thank you' card for you)
- A smiley face (someone cheering you up with a smile)

Assembly outline

If this assembly is being used to tie in with Valentine's Day, ask the children what special day it is today. Show them the Valentine's card and explain that some people feel very happy on Valentine's Day because they receive a card telling them that somebody loves them. However, some people can feel sad because they don't receive a card.

Say that when you were thinking about this, you suddenly realised that people do things every single day which show that they love you, so it doesn't matter at all whether anyone sends you a card on one particular day of the year.

Explain that you are going to show the children some objects that remind you that lots of people care about you. You want the children to guess what each of these objects is showing.

Invite a volunteer to come forward to hold the mug. Ask how a mug can show that someone loves you. Use your own explanation: it could be that someone brings you a cup of tea in bed, or a member of staff makes you a surprise cup of tea when you are on playground duty, or a friend takes you out for a cup of coffee to cheer you up.

Show the picture of a hug and demonstrate the action, if you like. Ask the children how this could make you feel loved. Explain that sometimes, when we are feeling sad, a hug can make us feel much better. Even when we feel happy, a hug can show us that someone cares about us.

Repeat for each of the objects, pointing out how each one shows that somebody cares.

Ask the children if they can think of other examples from their own lives which show them that someone cares. Examples could be a parent making them food, a grandparent reading them stories, a friend asking them to play or someone taking care of them when they fall over.

Explain that although Valentine's Day might be a good reminder to us of the importance of telling people that we care about them, every day gives us the opportunity to do so.

This assembly works well if the children have an opportunity to record their thanks to people who care for them. At the end of the assembly, in class after the assembly or at some point during the day, they could be allowed to write a sentence on a small piece of paper, saying 'thank you' to someone who has shown them love and care. Examples could be: 'Thank you, Mum, for making my bed'; 'Thank you, Harry, for being my friend'; 'Thank you, Grandad, for all the sweets.' Younger children could draw a picture or simply write a name. The papers could be used to make a display.

Small pieces of coloured card or paper look effective if they are arranged to spell out the word 'thank you' on a display board (one letter on each card) or if they are hung on a branch to make a 'thank you' tree.

What the Bible says

The Bible has a lot to say about love. It tells us that God loves us very much. In fact, **1 John 4:8** says that 'God is love'. **John 3:16** tells us that God loved us so much that he sent Jesus into the world to die for us, so that we could be forgiven: 'For God so loved the world that he gave his one and only Son.'

Not only does the Bible say that God loves us; it also tells us that we should love other people. In **John 13:34– 35**, Jesus says, 'A new commandment I give you: love one another. As I have loved you, so you must love one another.' **Matthew 5:44** tells us that we should love our enemies and pray for those who hurt us.

Pause for thought

Can you think of someone who has shown you in some way that they love you? Have you ever said 'thank you' to that person? Even if you haven't said 'thank you', have you shown by your actions that you are grateful? Is there someone you care about to whom you could show love today?

PRAYER
Dear God, thank you for all the people who show us love. Please help us never to take that love for granted but to say 'thank you' in our words and actions. Please help us to look for opportunities to show others that we care for them. Amen

50

World Book Day: books and reading

Aim: To encourage the children in their love of reading.

This assembly works well as an introduction to a charity event aimed at helping children in poorer areas of the world to receive an education or providing books for children in these areas.

You will need: Three of your favourite illustrated children's books aimed at younger readers; five staff members and their favourite children's books (prearranged); a Bible.

If possible, your favourite books should be familiar to the children. Make sure you collect the staff members' books from them before the assembly.

Assembly outline

If the assembly is being used in conjunction with World Book Day or a similar event, ask the children what is special about the day and explain its significance.

Ask if any of the children have a favourite book. Invite a few of them to share why they like these particular books. You may wish to prearrange this with a number of children so that they can bring their books to the assembly.

Say that you have brought three of your favourite children's books with you today. Show the children the three books and ask if anyone has read them. Explain that you are going to tell the children briefly about the books and show them the illustrations. After that, you will want them to vote for their favourite out of the three books. Say that if the children have already read the books, they can vote for the one they know is their favourite, but if they haven't read the books, you want them to vote for the one they would most like to read. (If time allows, you may like to read the most popular book to the children, or perhaps it could be read in each class during the school day.)

Point out that there are thousands of books in the world to choose from and everyone has their own ideas about what they prefer. Say that, before the assembly, you asked five staff members to select their favourite children's book. Show all these books to the children and explain, in a few sentences, what each book is about. After each summary, ask if any of the children are familiar with the story.

Ask the five staff members to come to the front and explain that you want the children to try to match the book with the adult who chose it. You could invite a volunteer to hand the books out to the adults and, if they have guessed incorrectly, ask a different volunteer to have a go until the books have been correctly distributed. Alternatively, you may prefer to ask all the children to vote on which staff member prefers which book.

Emphasise that it is a great privilege to be able to read and to have such a huge selection of books to choose from. Remind the children that there are many people in the world who have never had the opportunity to learn to read. Over 250 million children cannot read, which is more than a third of all the children in the world. Explain that many of these children live in poorer areas of the world, where they don't go to school. The fact that these children are not able to read can stop them getting jobs, which means that it is difficult for them to earn money. If these children were helped to get an education, it would make a huge difference to their lives.

If appropriate, introduce the children to the charity that is providing books or helping children to learn to read in poorer areas of the world.

Remind the children that all of us have different talents. Some of us find reading easy, while some of us find it more difficult. However, it is something that is worth persevering with, as it is not only useful in the future but also opens up hours of enjoyment.

What the Bible says

The Bible is thought to be the bestselling book of all time, with over five billion copies sold. It is divided into two main sections, called the Old and New Testaments. The Old Testament tells us about the time before Jesus was born and the New Testament tells us about Jesus' birth, life, death and resurrection and the start of the Christian church. The Bible is written by lots of different authors, and is made up of lots of separate books. Christians believe that God inspired people to write these books so that we can all know about him.

Pause for thought

Close your eyes and think about a book that you like to read. Why do you like that book? Maybe it's a fiction book and you like to get lost in the story; maybe it's an illustrated book and you love to look at the pictures; maybe it's a non-fiction book and you love to find out new facts and information about different topics. Whatever books you prefer, we are fortunate to have such a wide range available to us. Pause for a moment to be grateful that we have been given the opportunity to learn to read and to have a good education. Do we make the most of all the opportunities we are given?

PRAYER

Dear God, thank you for our school. Thank you that we have the opportunity to learn to read and that we are surrounded by so many books that we can enjoy. Please be with children all over the world who do not have the opportunities that we have. Please help us to do everything that we can to help them. Amen

Other books from
Barnabas in Schools...

KS1–2 / P1–7

36 Ready-to-Read
Assemblies for
Collective
Worship

**Taking your school through
the Bible story in a year**

Helen Lings

ISBN 978 0 85746 375 3
£9.99

*36 key Bible passages are covered in a year, each
accompanied by a ready-prepared thought for
the day, interactive questions, a prayer and a
song suggestion. Each assembly offers a choice
of traditional and contemporary versions of the
Bible.*

ISBN 978 0 85746 121 6
£9.99

Provides teaching material to help children explore moral and ethical issues around money. Includes ten story-led lesson plans with Bible links and cross-curricular classroom activities, plus three outlines for Collective Worship.

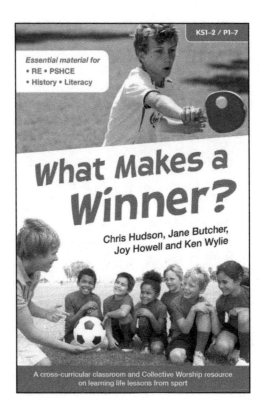

KS1–2 / P1–7

Essential material for
• RE • PSHCE
• History • Literacy

What Makes a Winner?

Chris Hudson, Jane Butcher,
Joy Howell and Ken Wylie

A cross-curricular classroom and Collective Worship resource
on learning life lessons from sport

ISBN 978 1 84101 742 6
£6.99

*Helps children to see beyond 'success' and
'winning' to deeper questions of behaviour,
citizenship and faith. Containing five lesson
plans and two assembly outlines, it uses stories
of inspirational athletes to teach PSHE values
such as friendship, equality and overcoming
difficulties.*

ISBN 978 1 84101 691 7
£8.99

Provides ten units of classroom material and three assemblies for 5–11s based on the theme of World War I. Each unit includes background information, an imaginative retelling of a real-life event, and cross-curricular activities.

Enjoyed

this book?

Write a review—we'd love to hear what you think.
Email: reviews@brf.org.uk

Keep up to date—receive details of our new books as they happen.
Sign up for email news and select your interest groups at:
www.brfonline.org.uk/findoutmore/

Follow us on Twitter @brfonline

By post—to receive new title information by post (UK only), complete the form below and post to: BRF Mailing Lists, 15 The Chambers, Vineyard, Abingdon, Oxfordshire, OX14 3FE

Your Details
Name _____
Address_____
_____
Town/City _____ Post Code _____
Email _____

Your Interest Groups (*Please tick as appropriate)	
❑ Advent/Lent	❑ Messy Church
❑ Bible Reading & Study	❑ Pastoral
❑ Children's Books	❑ Prayer & Spirituality
❑ Discipleship	❑ Resources for Children's Church
❑ Leadership	❑ Resources for Schools

Support your local bookshop
Ask about their new title information schemes.